Y MOMENT
OF A
FALL

A MEMOIR OF RECOVERY THROUGH EMDR THERAPY

CAROL E. MILLER

SCHAFFNER PRESS
Tucson, AZ

Library of Congress Cataloging-in-Publication Data

Names: Miller, Carol E., 1963-
Title: Every moment of a fall : a memoir of recovery through EMDR therapy /
  Carol E. Miller.
Description: First hardcover edition. | Tucson, AZ : Schaffner Press, Inc.,
  2016.
Identifiers: LCCN 2016010634 (print) | LCCN 2016011828 (ebook) | ISBN
  9781943156047 (hardback) | ISBN 9781943156054 (PDF) | ISBN 9781943156061
  (Epub) | ISBN 9781943156078 (Mobipocket)
Subjects: LCSH: Miller, Carol E., 1963- | Eye movement desensitization and
  reprocessing. | Desensitization (Psychotherapy) | Psychotherapy. |
  Aircraft accidents--Psychological aspects. | Airplane crash
  survival--Psychological aspects. | BISAC: BIOGRAPHY & AUTOBIOGRAPHY /
  Personal Memoirs. | PSYCHOLOGY / Psychotherapy / General.
Classification: LCC RC489.E98 M55 2016 (print) | LCC RC489.E98 (ebook) | DDC
  616.85/210651--dc23
LC record available at http://lccn.loc.gov/2016010634

For Andy,
every word

Author's Note

In writing this book, I've drawn largely on personal journals and correspondence as well as recordings of my EMDR therapist reading from her notes. This work is in no way intended to present a clinical overview of the full EMDR protocol. I have reconstructed my therapy experience from the point of view of a patient and storyteller, compressing, combining or reordering some sessions while leaving out others. At times I've approximated or guessed at what patient and therapist said to one another. And I have changed or omitted names when it seemed appropriate.

The Puritans, to keep the remembrance of their unity one with another . . . named their forest settlement Concord.

Ralph Waldo Emerson

Heaven is not like flying or swimming,
But has something to do with blackness and a strong glare.

Elizabeth Bishop

EVERY
MOMENT
OF A
FALL

1.
DEBRIS FIELD

"MOVE YOUR LEGS. CAROL, move your legs."

Ripples on a dark pool. A voice calling from the mouth of a cave. "I see your feet," it insists. "Now move your legs."

I swim toward the command in slow motion. My head plods to turn the words into some kind of action. At last it connects. I kick my legs.

"OK. Now get out." It's Dad's voice, barking. "Get out!"

My arm. It's wrenched behind me. I reach for my shoulder. Something hard is in the way. Something heavy, pressing. My arm is gone, underneath the pressing. It won't pull free.

"Carol, get out. Now! Get out!"

Daddy, I can't!

Light shining in my eyes. A shock of white hair behind it. A voice with a thick Boston accent asking questions. What's my name? How old am I? What day is this? I paddle toward it with stronger strokes.

"Am I in a car?" I ask.

"You're in a plane," the voice answers. "There's been an accident."

How long have I been lying outside in the dark? A fistful of wet dirt. The stink of gasoline. Soaking my hair and clothes. It's on my skin. I taste it when I close my lips to swallow. I'm in a plane?

My mind breaks the surface, gasping. There's been an accident!

A hatless man in uniform is pointing a flashlight at me. It's Sunday. We were flying home from Maine. There are dry leaves everywhere, rasping under the heels of my boots. My name is Carol. I'm sixteen.

"My arm!" I wail. "I can't get out."

Muffled bellowing of orders. The man crawls backwards out of the plane to talk with someone. He brings back more questions. Can I feel my fingers? Can I move my trapped hand? What is it touching? Can I reach any part of that arm with my free hand? And then, while we mark time, what grade am I in at the high school? What subjects do I like? Does Mrs. Graham still teach social studies? When he runs out of things to ask, he takes my free hand and assures me it will be all right. They're going to get me out.

Deep needles of pain gouge up and down my arm as the pressure suddenly releases. Blood lunges for my fingertips. Somebody somewhere grabs my numb hand and holds on with a too-tight grip. I tell my hatless man I can feel someone squeezing my hand, and he shouts to the ones outside. A spontaneous cheer erupts. My man tells me they have used the Jaws of Life to pry the crumpled nose of the plane apart. I don't know what the Jaws of Life is. I imagine the giant, skeletal head of a Tyrannosaurus Rex spitting me out of its mouth.

"We've got a stretcher," he says. "We're going to lift you. Nice and easy."

I protest. I can crawl out by myself. I'm too much for them to carry. He looks me full in the face and promises me one last time that everything will be all right.

They haul me feet first into the blaze of light trained on the crash site. The crowd sends up a collective gasp. The spotlight of a TV camera flashes on, over the shoulders of the paramedics. They load me fast into the waiting ambulance, like sliding me into a padded envelope. Everything goes silent. I sense that I should honor the hush, but I'm bursting to tell someone. This is my first time in an ambulance. My voice registers too loud in the bright quiet. The attendant smiles and nods.

The ride is fast and smooth. We are speeding along roads I know, but I can't picture the route.

•

IN THE EMERGENCY ROOM I am transferred again, from stretcher to gurney. A swarm of people in scrubs cuts me out of my clothes. There's a flurry of talk, but no one speaks to me. I feel a strong tug and my feet release both boots at once. The metal edge of a scissor runs up the inside of my thigh. I tense, remembering that I have my period. I should say something. I close my eyes and wait for them to discover the maxi pad in my underpants. There is a pause, then the cutting continues around it. Only the pad is left, anchored to nothing. They pull back my eyelids to shine light in my pupils. They dab blood from my hairline, tug stitches through the skin of my forehead. Someone covers my naked torso with a paper hospital gown. I count the seven, eight, nine times a nurse tries to insert an IV needle before giving up and calling a doctor. He waves her aside and spanks my arm to raise a vein.

Now another doctor is beside the first. I know he is a doctor because he wears a lab coat over his scrubs and addresses me directly. The pastor of our church slips into the room. All three men take a step closer and hunch their shoulders toward me at once. The second doctor delivers a brisk rundown of the casualties, best scenario to worst. He tells me Dad has been stabilized and is currently in surgery, but he should be fine. He tells me Mom is in Intensive Care, having hemorrhaged excessively. It's touch and go for her. He tells me Nancy didn't make it. He asks if I understand what he's said. I nod my head. The pastor brings his face very close to mine, mouthing how sorry he is, how very sorry. I realize I'm cold. I spot a blanket on a far chair. A nurse comes in just at that moment and asks if I want her to cover me. I nod, dumb with gratitude. The room empties. I'm alone under the white light.

Rolling down a corridor on my back, one orderly at my head, one steering my feet. Two sets of wheels bump over the threshold of an elevator. The bright hum as we rise, then two sets of wheels bump out. There are colored construction paper footprints taped to the ceiling. I track them to the nurses' station.

The staff on the Children's Ward are not happy about receiving a teenaged patient. I don't belong here, among the tonsillectomies and scarlet fever cases. I pretend not to hear the hushed argument taking place. My escorts insist there is no-where else to put me. The hospital is full, and the doctors have no reason to hold me in Intensive Care with my parents. But they can't release me either. Head trauma has to be watched for twenty-four to forty-eight hours.

"This is it," one of them hisses. "There's nothing else available." A nurse squeaks away to ready a bed.

I try not to wince as they heave me from the gurney into cold, starched sheets. The three other beds are empty. There's an orange plastic water pitcher on the nightstand and a metal bedpan waiting on the tray table. A nurse warns that under no circumstances am I to get out of bed, even to take the ten steps to the bathroom. She reminds me that I am tethered to an IV drip. She shows me the call button and instructs me to use it if I need something. The way she says this makes it clear that I am to need nothing, that my presence will be tolerated as long as I don't make a nuisance of myself. There are far more important things to attend to on the Children's Ward than a girl whose X-rays show no injuries. A girl whose legs already reach the end of the bed.

Our youth group leader from church, Buddy, has been wait-ing to see me. A second-year seminarian, he's not much older than I am. He has Southern manners and a sensitive streak that I like. He sits leaning into the circle of light cast by the reading lamp. His face is shiny with tears that keep coming and that he does not wipe away. He holds my hand and says simple things. How horribly sad it is that this has happened. How grateful he is that I'm alive. How he almost feels guilty saying so, since Nancy is dead. I watch him through eyes swollen to slits. He goes on crying and holding my hand. It feels like the sky behind him, outside the window, has always been this black.

The nurse returns to end our visit, bringing pills in a doll-sized paper cup. I swallow them one by one. She crumples the cup and switches off the lamp. Night closes over me like a heavy lid.

The dark is laden with fragments. A voice, a pair of hands, a child bawling in another room. At what must be hourly intervals, a thumb draws my eyelids open, first the right, then the left. A laser of light slices into each pupil. A hand circles my wrist. Two fingers probe for a pulse. My mind claws through thick fur to come awake. I heave myself up to swallow another round of pills. There is the same series of questions. What is your name? How old are you? Where do you live? What year is this? Who is the president? Each time, just as I shake myself fully awake, the flashlight snaps off and the interrogator is gone. My heart balls into a fist and pounds to get out. Alone! Alone! Alone!

•

FAITH, THE DAY NURSE, appears soon after sunrise and introduces herself. She is plainspoken and looks me in the eyes. She tells me how sorry she is for what I've been through. She busies herself straightening the bed linens and clearing away the empty cups and chaos of the night shift. She brings me a no-chew breakfast. I'm not hungry, but she lingers beside the bed, so I try. I realize I haven't eaten since yesterday afternoon. We were all there together, at my brother's house, chewing and chewing. Nancy flitting from perch to perch because she can't—she couldn't—sit still. I close my eyes against the thrumming in my head and slump back against the pillows. I want my mother.

Faith continues to ease me through the routine tasks of a day. First we eat, then we pee. She slips the bedpan beneath the blanket. I tell her I don't have to go, but she asks me to try anyway. A hot stream of urine wets my inner thigh and spills onto the sheet. She wipes my leg with a hand towel and maneuvers around me in the bed, pulling off the wet bedding and replacing it without standing me up.

"Don't worry," she says. "It happens all the time."

She disappears for several minutes and comes back with an old-fashioned maxi pad, the kind with a belt and garter clips.

"This is all I could find," she apologizes. She helps me rig it up between my legs. The pill tray comes around, carried in the daytime by a jittery candy striper. Faith watches me swallow the contents of the little pleated paper cup. "It's been a busy morning," she says. She tells me to relax and she'll be back after I've had a rest.

I wake woozy from medicated sleep. My head throbs. My arm throbs. My shoulders, ribs, neck, nose, eyelids. Everything pulses and aches. Faith returns. She sets a stack of towels on the bedside table and pulls a comb and a travel-size bottle of shampoo out of her pocket. She steps out into the hallway again and comes back with a plastic basin and an extra water pitcher. She assures me I will feel much better with clean hair. She fills two pitchers in the bathroom sink. Then she levels the bed, lifts my head off the pillows and lowers it gently into the basin. As she pours warm water over my temples and scalp, she explains that the head likes to bleed.

"A lot," she says. "It really puts on a show."

She uses the comb to start easing knots out of each hank of hair. She treats one section at a time, without yanking.

"You have so much pretty hair," she tells me, and it doesn't sound like a veiled complaint, like she wishes she could skip this chore.

We go through four changes of rust-colored water. She offers the basin for inspection each time before walking it to the bathroom and dumping the contents down the toilet. The water is no less bloodied after the final rinse, but Faith seems satisfied. She gently wrings my hair in a towel, then spreads a fresh one over my pillow. She gathers the pitchers and wet towels in the basin and tells me to relax while my hair dries.

"I have something to show you," she announces after lunch, spreading a clean towel on the tray table.

Like a scientist displaying specimens, she arranges, one by one, the things that washed out of my hair. They fall into two categories: natural and manmade. On one half of the tray she lays out what looks like the makings of an entire bird's nest. Big twigs, smaller sticks and dry leaves, all of which have absorbed the color of head blood and the smell of airplane fuel, acrid and tart. I blink my eyes but the stink won't clear.

On the other half of the tray she arrays the manmade items. There are stubby machine screws, a pair of toothpick-sized springs, shards of safety glass and a handful of metallic bits that serve some purpose neither of us can guess. Faith encourages me to look at each item, to pick it up and judge its weight, to theorize what its function might have been. It's all very matter-of-fact. First we learned how badly the head can bleed: after four assays, there was no diminishment in the amount of blood staining the rinse water. Now we're determining the volume of objects that can be concealed in human hair. These are the lessons for the day.

My siblings begin arriving. Sue and Bruce have flown home from college in the middle of the semester. Our half-brothers Tedd and Allon have ducked out of their jobs for a few days, leaving their own kids to be with us. Seeing Sue, especially, is a relief, like fingering a smooth stone in my pocket. But her eyes are spooked. She was allowed to see Mom for a minute before coming up here. Just looking has drained all the blood from her face. Bruce tries to cheer me up. He tells me that Nancy is laughing and singing with Jesus in heaven. My older brothers bring the same message, Tedd with a Bible open on his lap, Allon with sad eyes and fatherly ways. Somebody suggests that God took Nancy so young to spare her further pain. Her difficult childhood would have meant a troubled adolescence and adulthood, too much to bear.

It gets hard to listen. My eyelids are cardboard. My arm prickles with the phantom stings of a hundred bees. My head feels like it's packed inside a steel cage. Each heartbeat slams my forehead against the bars.

A nurse wheels a little boy wearing *Star Wars* pajamas to the bed across from mine. His mother bends over him and ruffles his hair, reminding him brightly that he's allowed to eat all the ice cream he wants. Then she straightens and whispers something to the nurse. The two women turn to look at me with alarm. I close my eyes, but I still feel them looking.

People from church come for visiting hours. Kids from school show up after classes. Everyone winces when they walk into the room. One girl bursts into tears and has to step into the hallway. She returns dry-eyed but no less shaky. My friends tell me I made the eleven o'clock news. The church people talk about God's will. Standing stiffly beside the bed in woolen layers, they all complain about how warm it is on the Children's Ward.

"I know," I say. "Sorry."

The nurse comes back to check on my roommate, the boy with the ice cream, and I hear her mutter that the line of visitors in the corridor stretches almost to the elevator. Now there are fewer familiar faces. Most of the people streaming through the room are strangers.

"Your father saved my life," one tells me.

Another says, "The fall was so bad my brother couldn't walk or speak afterward. But your father brought him back to us."

A woman announces that she finally had a baby last month after trying for years. "Your father is a miracle worker," her husband says.

Everyone wants me to get a message to Dad. Be sure to tell him that Jerry, Paula, John and Pat, Smitty and the Stewart family came by. That Chad and Muff, Sissy, June and Jim are praying for him. That Heidi, Charles and Charlie Sr. want to know what they can do to help. One of them says when she heard about the crash on the news, she couldn't believe it was her own doctor the reporters were talking about. She had to see him right away, to make sure he was all right. But when she got to the hospital they told her that, on the critical wards downstairs, only immediate family were permitted to visit.

Apparently there are no such restrictions on the Children's Ward. It seems like anybody's allowed up here. So Dad's visitors file through my room instead of his. Each one has a story to tell, and each story ends with the tremendous debt of gratitude they owe him for making them well. When they're done speaking, they look at me expectantly. Good manners oblige me to respond. I smile and nod reassuringly. I tell them Dad's going to be fine. I make certain not to cry, my dry eyes underscoring this message. Everything is going to be just fine.

•

"IF YOU FINISH YOUR breakfast," Faith promises on my second morning in the hospital, "you can walk to the bathroom on your own. No more bedpan." With that incentive, I choke down most of the smooth food on my tray.

After the candy striper makes her rounds, Faith helps me swing my legs over the side of the bed and sit up. "Do you feel light-headed?" she wants to know. I tell her no, but we rest for a minute anyway. She wheels the IV pole close enough for me to grasp it with my good hand. "Use this to keep your balance," she says. "Don't lean on it, just hold yourself steady." I pitch forward and hoist myself to my feet. The hospital gown falls open in back and I reach around to close the gap with my free hand. Pain sparks up my arm. I gasp as my shoulder bursts into flame. Faith lays a hand on the small of my back. "I've got you," she says.

We stand for a moment. "How does that feel?" she asks. I nod. "I'm going to let go now," she says and pulls her hand away. I shuffle the ten steps to the bathroom door. "I'll wait right here," Faith says behind me. "Just say my name if you need me."

I pull the door until it latches, then turn toward the toilet, my gaze catching in the mirror above the sink. It takes several seconds to make sense of the thing reflected there, the scrambled fragments of a face. Eyes pushed to the sides of my head. Nose, mouth and chin swollen to four times their normal size and thrust forward. The whole mess framed by blood-dark ropes of hair. I lunge for the low seat and land hard, ducking my head between my knees. A gorgon-headed, fish-faced girl trying not to faint on a kiddie toilet.

Faith calls through the door, "All right in there?" I lift my head and fight to steady my voice. "I'm OK."

It takes a few more breaths for the dizziness to pass. I sit upright, unhook the belted maxi pad and force out a stream of pee. I struggle up to standing, glad for the IV pole to hold onto. I re-hook the belt and step to the sink, bracing myself for another look at my face. Chin jutting out like an elbow beneath my mouth. Maroon and purple and violet rings smudged like greasepaint around each puffed slit of an eye. A column of X-shaped stitches stacked from my right eyebrow into my hairline. Bottom lip split. I turn my head slowly, considering each side. It is hard to find a single patch of normal, flesh-colored skin.

"Bruising looks terrible," Faith says when I emerge. "But it's only temporary." This must be the lesson for today. Lowering myself back onto the bed, I turn the wrong way and get looped in the plastic tubing. She stands me up again and frees the line, then holds it aside while I slide beneath the covers. She smoothes the sheet under my chin, tells me to rest and leaves the room. But she comes right back, carrying a hand mirror. She sets it face down on the bedside table and says, "Whenever you're ready."

·

A BABY SCREAMS THROUGH the night, then goes silent. When Faith arrives with my breakfast tray, I tell her the screaming woke me. She explains that the baby came in with a high fever. They did everything they could to bring it down, but he was too small and too sick to fight off the infection. He died just before dawn.

After I eat and pee and swallow my pills, Faith wheels a little girl to my bedside. She is oddly twisted, as if her body grew by twining itself around the trunk of a tree. Faith sets a short stack of books on my tray table and asks me to read aloud. I don't know how long we sit there, an almost-grown girl filling a hospital bed and a small, spiral girl in a wheelchair smiling through each page.

When Faith comes to take my visitor back to her room, I can tell something has changed. She returns with the empty wheelchair and says she has some good news. Because I'm doing so well, there's no reason to keep me another night. I'll be leaving the hospital this afternoon.

"But first," she says, "you're going to visit your mother and father. I'll help you get ready."

My heart curls up like it's been kicked. I don't want to get ready. I don't want to see my parents. I want to stay right here with Faith. Why can't I? She volunteers the little information she has. A friend of the family is coming to pick me up after lunch. I'll be staying with her for a while, until my parents are strong enough to take me home.

"Do I have to?" I ask.

"Have to what?"

"Do I have to go see them?"

"Your mother must be very worried. She needs to see for herself that you're all right."

"Will you come with me?"

Faith can't leave the ward, but she has asked Mike, her favorite orderly, to take me downstairs. She promises I'll be fine. She pulls my purple chenille bathrobe from the skinny closet by the bed and maneuvers me into it. It's too painful to move my right arm more than a few degrees in any direction, so she starts there, guiding the sleeve up past my elbow and over my shoulder. She knots the belt around my waist. She draws my hair out from beneath the collar and tucks a few loose, blood-crusted strands behind my ear.

"There," she says. "You look nice. Ready?"

Leaving the room is strange. As Mike rolls me down the corridor, people pass without noticing, pivoting out of the path of the chair. I check the ceiling while we're waiting for the elevator. The colored footprints are still there.

Mom's room is scarier than I imagined. There is a nest of rubber tubing, a plastic tent over part of the bed and a stack of blinking machinery, some of it mounted to the ceiling. She's flat on her back with clear tubes and something that looks like a vacuum cleaner hose stuck into her side. Her head is wrapped in gauze, her left eye covered with a patch. She is tiny lying there.

Mike hands me off to an ICU nurse, who wheels me up to the bed and bends down to whisper, "She can hear you. Go ahead." But I've forgotten how to breathe, let alone speak. I reach for Mom's hand, bloodless against the sheet. Her fingers twitch. She turns her head slowly, dragging it through congealed air. Her gaze lands on my chest, groggy and unfocused, and travels to my face. She pulls fiercely awake. Her words come hoarse and panting, in a surprising rush.

"Carol," she says. "I'm so thankful this happened to me and not to you. You'll be able to find a husband, get married." She struggles to swallow, then begins to cry.

"Mom," I say.

"Oh honey," she says, "God has a wonderful plan for your life. That's why He spared you. To do something great."

The nurse comes running, summoned by a honking alarm. She clamps a mask over Mom's mouth and nose. My heart pitches in my chest like a rubber raft. I hold tight to Mom's gaze as Mike wheels me backwards out of the room.

There are no machines or monitors or flashing lights in Dad's room. Just two beds, the far one empty. His chest is wound tight with bandages. His right arm is in a cast that runs all the way to his shoulder. There's a pulley on the ceiling with a rope attached to his sling. His arm has to stay raised. Every morning they hoist it up again.

He wants to tell me what he remembers. The radio exchange with Hanscom control on approach, seeing the lights below, waking up in the baggage hold.

"We traded places," he tells me, his voice flat. "You came forward into the cockpit. I wound up aft. I asked you to move your legs. I knew we had to get out. My throttle arm was useless, though. I could see the hand flopping at the wrist, barely attached. Between that and these busted ribs, I couldn't move."

I close my eyes. My head pulses. Dad keeps going.

"Nan was still strapped in," he says. "Hanging upside-down."

Faith helps me gather my things in a grocery bag. I'll leave the magazines, but I need to keep the Get Well cards. Sue dropped off some clothes earlier. Faith eases my bad arm into the sleeve of my yellow sweater and pulls it over my head. I ball up my purple robe and stuff it into the bag. Faith asks if she can give the flower arrangements to some of the other kids on the ward. I nod. She stands facing me for a long moment. She tells me I'd better come visit her. I nod again. She tells me I'm going to be all right. "Better than all right," she says, and gives me a quick hug.

Vi Frizzell arrives to pick me up. Faith tells me I have to leave the hospital in a wheelchair. She walks with us to the elevator. Vi pushes me inside and the doors bump shut. I wait in the lobby while she drives her car around to the front.

I climb into the passenger seat and catch myself digging for the seatbelt. I wasn't wearing one on the plane. I remember unbuckling it and folding forward to nap. Pulling my trench coat over my head like a hood. Nancy pinching my leg. Me slapping her hand away. Lifting my coat to glare at her.

I cinch the belt tight across my lap, tight enough to bite into my thighs.

The hospital parking lot is across the street from the country club Dad joined so he could play golf after work. Nancy and I spent most of last summer there, in the pool. When thunderstorms rolled through the humid afternoons, we jumped out and huddled wet in the locker room until the lifeguard gave the signal that it was safe to get back in the water.

Vi makes a right out of the parking lot. We drive through leaf-littered streets on a Wednesday afternoon, the town center scrolling by like a movie. We overtake the high school cross-country team running in a tight pack. We pass the street where a friend from junior high lives, now that her parents are divorced. In the Friendly's parking lot, there's a clutch of senior boys leaning against a pickup truck. We pass moms coming home from the grocery store or the hair salon, or carpooling to the soccer game. Jack-o'-lanterns grin from flagstone steps. "It's Halloween," I tell Vi, doing the math, and right away I feel stupid. She knows what day it is.

•

STEPPING INTO VI'S KITCHEN, I get the first whiff of home in days, even if it isn't my own. It smells of casseroles, of ground beef and tomato, green pepper and macaroni. The smell hasn't changed in all the years I've been coming here. I sit at the big table while she makes me a cup of tea. I hear the boys slam in from the school bus. They greet the dogs in the basement, pound noisily up the steps and spill into the kitchen, all skinny limbs and sharp angles. One is my age, one a year younger, the youngest Nancy's age. They pull up short when they see me at the table, while the dogs continue to weave excitedly between them. The boys look down sheepishly, not knowing what to say. Nancy is dead for them, too.

Our growing up together hangs in the casserole-smelling air between us. All the Christmas Eves. All the trips out to dinner in church clothes. While the rest of us kids plundered the relish tray, Nancy would dart between the bathroom and the front register, taking mints from the bowl or toothpicks from the dispenser. Our families spent one Easter vacation together in Florida. We kids sprinted back and forth across the same stretch of beach, trying to outrun the waves, while adults on the pool deck above us drank cocktails. "Y'all have gas?" we shrieked to each other for seven days straight, mimicking Vi's southern drawl.

The dogs begin to whine. The boys break into motion again, racing from the kitchen to prepare for a school-night Halloween.

Vi draws me a bath before dinner. I slide into the foam, close my eyes and pray for the water to unhook me from my body. Chin deep in the soapy warmth, I pretend that everything's normal again. I picture Nancy tiptoeing up to the closed bathroom door and switching off the light from the outside, just to hear me holler. A hard knot cinches in my throat. The throb of my arm and shoulder won't let me slip my skin. I don't want the smell of Cashmere Bouquet or the nubby softness of the wash cloth against my neck. I raise myself with one arm, unstop the drain and step out of the tub. I let my purple robe finish drying the places I can't reach.

After dinner the house empties. Vi goes upstairs to tend to something in one of the bedrooms. The desk lamp is on in Al's study, where he usually spends the evening. But he's not there. He could be at the hospital visiting my parents. Or maybe he's helping Sue sort through the mess of Dad's medical practice, on hold until he gets well.

I wander the rooms on the ground floor, still in my robe. There are shelves with tchotchkes and books that must have always been there, but they seem unfamiliar. There's a bowl of candy at the ready by the front door, although no one expects trick-or-treaters in this part of town. The houses are too far apart, the driveways too long, the roads too dark. I unwrap a peanut butter cup, thankful that Vi went for the good stuff. The sudden chiming of the doorbell startles me. I listen for movement in the upstairs hallway, for treads on the stairs. Nothing happens. The door chimes again. I move through the living room and cross the foyer to answer it, reaching for the candy bowl with my left hand as the right one works the lock. A woman and a very small boy are standing on the stoop.

"Trick or treat!" they call out in unison, then stiffen when they see me.

They were expecting someone else. I explain that Vi is upstairs, I'm not sure where. She must not have heard the door. The woman tells me they're neighbors. They live in the little house on the corner of Brook Street. I tell her I'm a friend staying with the family for a while.

"I love your costume," the woman says. "Great makeup! The bruising even matches your robe."

She squats down beside her son in his store-bought Superman outfit and whispers to him not to be afraid, it's just pretend. She glances back up at me, grinning conspiratorially. I dump half of the candy from the bowl into the plastic pumpkin the boy is carrying like a purse. I tell them Vi will be sorry she missed them.

The next morning the boys head out to catch the school bus without me. I don't know when I'll be going back. How can I, with a face that scares little kids and makes my friends cry?

Vi is determined to wash the rest of the blood out of my hair. She pulls up a chair and helps me climb onto the kitchen counter. She has to clear away spice jars and glass canisters of pasta to make room for my full length. I stretch out on my back and lower my head slowly into the sink. She lets the faucet run until the water warms, but the first blast from the sprayer comes out cold against my scalp. She squeezes a glob of shampoo into her palm and starts scrubbing. It smells like Prell. She sees me wince and asks if it hurts. I say yes. She doesn't talk about what she's seeing, just continues to scrub hard with her fingernails. After she has lathered and rinsed and lathered and rinsed, she seems satisfied that the head blood is vanquished. She helps me climb down. We wrap my hair in a bath towel, winding it like a turban. I will begin to feel more like myself in no time, she assures me. I'm grateful. What she has done is tender, even if her touch is not.

When I drift into the kitchen later, my hair still damp at the nape of my neck, Vi and the woman who rang the doorbell last night are sitting at the table. There are china cups and a matching tea service between them. Vi introduces us and goes to fetch another cup and saucer from the dining room. I sit next to the neighbor. She covers my left hand with hers and tells me how terribly sorry she is for what she said to me at the door. She had no idea who I was. She lets a sob surface, then continues. She is mortified for making such a horrible mistake. But more than that, she says, she is so sorry for my loss. For how deeply I must be grieving my little sister. For how frightening it must be with my parents in the hospital. For how scary the crash must have been. She asks me to please come visit her any time, in the little house on the corner of Brook Street. Whenever I want to talk, she says, she'll be there.

I don't know her, but I feel safe next to her. While she and Vi gossip, I imagine laying my head on the table, right here between the teacups, pressing my cheek against the polished wood and letting this stranger stroke my clean hair.

•

MY HEAD IS A NORMAL size again. The swelling in my face has gone down and most of the bruises have disappeared. It's time to go back to school. Vi suggests I cover what's left of my black eye with makeup, but I don't. I have so little to show for what's happened. I want people to feel sorry for me.

Most kids say nothing to me in the halls. They whisper

when I've passed. Kids I've known since second grade avoid my eyes. Others, virtual strangers, startle me with their composure. The varsity cheerleader, the class president, the stoner kid from swim team all go out of their way to talk to me. They welcome me back. Some hand me cards filled with signatures and smiley faces. Some tell me how sorry they are and ask me to please come to them if there's anything they can do to help.

My teachers' responses are mixed, too. Some just nod to me when they take attendance. Others pull me aside in embarrassing displays. My physics teacher, who wears the same plaid polyester sports coat every day, asks the class to sit quietly while he and I step into his office. He tells me that I don't have to make up the work I've missed. I am not to worry about any of it, he says. I feel relieved. And beholden now to see him as a whole person. An English teacher I've never had lays a hand on my shoulder. He says it's nice to see my face brightening the halls again.

It's exhausting. The half-numb, half-crawling sensation beneath the skin of my right arm intensifies as the school day wears on. My shoulder thrums. I hold my throbbing head as still as possible on the bus ride back to Vi's. It's a different bus, so not many of the kids know me. I'm almost grateful to be left alone, staring stiffly out the window. My regular bus driver sent me a Get Well card with the words "school bus driver" in parenthesis under her signature. I bet she's actually relieved. All the mornings I've been away, she hasn't had to wait for me to sprint down the road at the last minute.

Not long after my return to school, I lug my book bag through the back door into Vi's kitchen and find Dad sitting at the table. The doctors released him early, maybe because he'd been such a nuisance. He insisted they move Mom out of the ICU into his room. The day after they made the transfer, she had a close call. One of her broken ribs slipped and re-punctured a lung. Blood and other gunk began to seep in and press out the air. She was drowning. There were no machines in Dad's room to breathe for her, or to sound the alarm. He kept leaning on the call button, but no one would respond. With his arm in traction, he couldn't get out of bed to save her. Finally a visitor came in, saw what was happening, ran down the corridor and grabbed the first nurse he could find. "A woman is dying!" he yelled. "Come quick!"

Dad spends his days at Vi's kitchen table wearing pajamas and his blue wool bathrobe, his feet in fleece-lined moccasins. As usual, he talks and talks and talks. When I get home from school, he sits me at the table while he goes over everything again. An FAA investigator has been asking questions, and Dad has to write a report of the flight. On final approach, he tells me, he saw landing lights below.

"But they must have been streetlights," he says. "They had to be. We were still too far out."

He doesn't remember hitting the throttle at that point, but he tells me that would have been procedure. The next thing he remembers is the tips of my cowboy boots, pointing up. Nancy's legs hanging down. He remembers calling to me. Asking me to move my feet. Telling me to get out. I sit at Vi's table in the fading afternoon light and listen as best I can. I understand that he needs to say these things, and I try to be the person he can say them to. He stares out the kitchen window, past the lawn in shadow to the thicket of trees beyond.

"You saved my life," he says. My head snaps up. "You saved my life," he repeats. "You told a resident in the ER that you weren't able to wake up and buckle your seatbelt when you felt the pressure changing in your ears."

I did? When?

"If you hadn't said that, they wouldn't have thought to test my blood for carbon monoxide. Hours after the crash, the level was still high. It must've leaked in through the heater. It knocked you kids out, and your mother. That explains the confusion with the streetlights, too, right before I went under."

Carbon monoxide? Like when you leave the car running with the garage door closed?

He goes on. "I wouldn't have been able to live with myself, believing that I'd killed her. I would have committed suicide. But now I don't have to. Now we know the gas did it. You saved my life."

I feel embarrassed for both of us. He's giving me credit for something I don't remember doing. I feel scooped out inside, too, because there's no gratitude in his voice. The words don't sound like praise, although he says them as if saving his life was the most important work a person could undertake. It feels like we're on stage together, Dad shaking my hand and smiling for the cameras as he passes me a plaque for lifesaving. Something tells me I'll be punished for all this. For intervening on his behalf. For being the person he momentarily relies upon to prove he's not at fault.

On the weekend, Vi's house is noisy with kids and adults and dogs, all of us in motion, circulating through the day around the fixed point of Dad at the kitchen table. Vi has taken the three boys down to the basement to cut their hair with electric clippers, and this gives Dad an idea. He is frantic for a haircut himself. He's used to reaching into his back pocket for a comb dozens of times a day. Now with his right arm in a sling and his left arm guarding still-tender ribs, he can't slick back the hanks of hair that keep falling over his eyes. He could ask Vi for a trim, while she's at it, but he asks me instead.

"I don't know how to cut hair," I tell him.

"How hard can it be?" he counters, and the implication is clear. Housewives can cut hair. Uneducated people with no better prospects in life can cut hair. If you can't even cut hair, Carol, what does that make you? I tell him that if I cut his hair it will look bad. He won't like it. He says he doesn't care what it looks like. He says all that matters to him is getting the hair out of his eyes.

We take the basement stairs slowly, pausing to land both feet on each tread. I'm ahead of him, inching down backwards in case he loses his footing. A beat-up chair from an old dining set sits in the center of a stained bed sheet, spread on the floor to catch what falls. There's a plastic cape to drape over his shoulders. I comb the hair straight down from the top of his head to see how much needs to go. I try to follow the line made by the barber before me, but it's hard to cut clean across his forehead. His hair is fine and lank. And slippery. Strands jump away from the scissors as I go. Because it won't lie still, I keep returning to the beginning of the line to try to even things up. I can't hold the comb level in my left hand, and my right hand with the scissors is starting to sweat. I step back and pretend to be studying my work like a person who knows what she's doing. But I'm flubbing it. Dad sputters away the fine hairs falling on his lips and makes the disapproving cluck in his throat that means, You idiot!

When I'm done, his bangs are like a row of uneven teeth. I brush the clippings away with my fingertips. I tell him to close his eyes and I blow a big puff of air across his forehead and down the bridge of his nose. I unsnap the barber cape and shake the hair onto the sheet beneath us. Then I hold up a cracked mirror so he can see what I've done.

He whistles. "You weren't kidding," he says. "You really don't know how to cut hair."

•

WHEN DAD GETS TIRED of sitting in Vi's kitchen, he trades his bathrobe and pajamas for khakis and a cardigan. There are things he needs to attend to. He asks Bruce to drive him to the Concord fire house so he can talk with the men who pulled us out of the plane. He wants to gather information, measure their version of events against his own and, of course, thank them for saving the lives they were able to save. He asks if I want to come along. I'm not sure, so I say yes.

The men seem surprised we've come but they're willing to talk. They shrug off praise, saying they were just doing their jobs, that anyone would have done the same. They take turns telling us what happened, based on what they saw firsthand

and what they pieced together afterwards. The plane dove into a stand of trees on the edge of the conservation area. The wings sheared off and the nose slammed down in someone's backyard. The family wasn't home at the time. The fuselage dug a trench across the lawn from the woods to the back wall of the empty house. The plane flipped upside-down, but the tail caught against the porch roof, which is probably why we weren't crushed inside. It was a dark, overcast night. People in the neighborhood heard a loud noise, like ice sliding off a roof, then nothing. Thirty minutes later a woman called the police to report a strong smell of gasoline. She told the responding officer that she'd been hearing what sounded like cries for help coming from the woods. He searched the area, spotted a trail of debris on a neighboring lawn and tracked it to the plane.

The men hesitate. They're wondering how much they should say. Dad asks about Nancy. They tell us they found her still belted into her seat, arms and legs dangling down into the flipped cabin. They quickly add that she must have died on impact.

"A child that size," the chief says. "With the belt around her waist, the force of the crash would have severed a main artery." He's sure she went instantly and didn't suffer. Dad nods.

One of the men says they almost stumbled over Mom, slumped against a tree a few feet from the plane. She must have been thrown clear of the wreckage.

"She wasn't thrown," Dad interrupts, explaining that he smelled fuel and knew the plane could blow, so he kept telling us to get out. Mom was the only one who managed it. She remembers wriggling out of the plane on her stomach and crawling to the tree. Dad tells them a surgery team spent hours tweezing mud and leaves and gravel out of the cavities around her knees.

The men admit I gave them a real scare. They couldn't figure out how to free my pinned arm. There was gasoline everywhere. A reporter showed up with a lit cigarette and three guys chased him back down the street. They figured it was just a matter of time before the plane exploded, so a surgery team was sent from the hospital to amputate my arm at the shoulder. Their ambulance pulled up to the crash site just as the Jaws of Life pried open the nose of the plane and set me loose. I rub my arm and picture a line of doctors filing out of an ambulance, each one carrying a black bag with scalpels glinting inside, ready to cut.

As we're leaving, a couple of the men say it's good to see us up and around and getting back to life. I'm not really back to anything. I haven't slept in my own bed for weeks. Mom is still in the hospital. Nancy hasn't been buried yet. But I say thank you anyway, because they saved my life.

•

I OVERHEAR THE ADULTS talking about Nancy's funeral. The funeral director checks daily to see if Mom's release date has been set. Everyone is worried that time is running out. There's going to be an open casket. The body has been embalmed, but even in cold storage it will soon be too decomposed for a viewing. The director asks Sue to choose burial clothes. She settles on the peach pantsuit. Nancy insisted on wearing it long after the pants came half-way up her shins. Sue asks if I think it's the right choice, and I do. I've already forgotten what she was wearing the day of the crash. Now when I picture her next to me on the plane, my mind dresses her in the peach pantsuit.

Word comes that Mom will be released for Thanksgiving. Dad decides that we can't all stay at Vi's, that we'll make do in our own house. It's not clear if Mom will be able to walk, much less climb the stairs to her bedroom. Both of her knees are slowly being reconstructed, since the crash sliced them open to the bone.

When Dad brings her home, she's wearing a black patch over her bandaged eye. She's had plastic surgery to reattach the left side of her face. The effort of just keeping her balance with one eye covered makes her nauseous. Getting washed and dressed for Thanksgiving dinner at Vi's exhausts her.

To make room for all of us, Vi has borrowed a few folding tables from church. Bruce and Sue are home again from college. My brother Tedd, his wife and their daughter drove down from Portland. She's just a few years younger than Nancy was. The two of them played together in Maine the day of the crash. As we scoot our chairs up to the makeshift table, I wonder if my niece senses the question hanging in the room. Why is this girl alive to play with her food, fidget in her chair, dive under the table to pick up her napkin? Why one girl and not the other?

Mom can't sit at the table. Her knees have to be elevated, so Vi sets her up in Al's recliner with bed pillows to cushion her ribs. I watch her over the bowed heads during Tedd's prayer of thanksgiving for the food, for the good fellowship of family and friends, for the precious life taken home to Jesus. She looks like a dazed bird swatted out of the sky.

The viewing is set for a few nights later. Our pastor encourages me to attend. Maybe he's the one who's been pushing all along for the open casket. It will bring closure, he promises. Mom isn't going after all. She says it's because she's not strong enough yet, but I heard Dad tell her he doesn't want her to go. He's not going. He says he doesn't need to see Nancy's body to get closure. He knows his daughter is dead.

At the funeral home, I wind up in the first row of folding chairs. Two old ladies sit with me, Grammy and her friend Marguerite, who we call Aunt Peggy. We don't talk. We stare straight ahead. The coffin is white. It's on a pedestal high enough to prevent me from seeing inside from this angle. When we came in, before an usher walked me to my seat, I caught a glimpse of Nancy's head in profile. Now all I can see is the side of the box. I wonder if someone is going to give me a signal to do what I'm supposed to. To get closure. Grammy leans over and whispers, "Maybe you shouldn't look."

The room is overly warm. It's decorated like a living room, with thick oriental rugs and pairs of wingback chairs. People are crying. Their faces crease and dissolve as they pause over the casket. Vi stands for a long time, head bowed. I imagine she is memorizing the features of a girl she helped raise. A girl whose face has already begun to erase itself. There's a break in the line. One beat, two beats, and without thinking it through I stand, then walk, skirting the foot of the white box, sidling toward the head on the pillow.

Close up, it's obvious this isn't Nancy. It couldn't be. First, the hair is all wrong. The center part is perfect. Each side sweeps neatly away from her face and lies stiff with hairspray. Second, the skin is fake, spray-tan orange like the big rubber doll they used in gym class to teach us mouth-to-mouth. Everything's wrong. Even her peach pantsuit against the satin fabric swirled around her.

The casket lid is in two sections, like the doors on a horse's stall. The lower section is closed, covering everything below her rib cage. They must not want us to see that part of her, especially the place where the seatbelt cut in. My hand goes into the box. I can't stop it. I need to touch her, on the shoulder first, with a fast recoil. Then over her heart, a few seconds longer. There's no difference between one spot and another. She feels like cement, all the softness sucked out of her. And she's cold. Much colder than my hand. The word "set" pops into my head. Set hard as blacktop, or plaster. Her expression is familiar, like someone doing an impression of her. Like a second layer of face has been stretched over her real face and sewn in place, the stitches hidden in her hairline. It's a corpse with the trappings of Nancy, but it's not her. I look up, aware for the first time that people are watching me. Deliberately staying away. Giving me time for goodbye. I should cry. Everyone else is crying. My sister is dead, replaced by a fake. I should cry.

We leave for the cemetery a few minutes before noon the next day. It's cold and threatening rain. I miss my trench coat. The one Mom made for me. The one I pulled over my head in the plane to block the light and fend off Nancy's pinches and pokes. It's not hard to spot the gravesite. There's a huge hearse parked in front of it, and a couple of men from the funeral home in black overcoats guarding a rectangular hole. Mom can barely walk from where we leave the car in the middle of a muddy lane. There's a carpet of kelly green Astroturf spread around the grave like a skirt. A low brass scaffold suspends the white coffin over the hole. The green of the Astroturf and the white of the coffin scream against the browns and grays of the day.

Just after the noon whistle blows at the fire station, the committal service begins. Because Mom can't be on her feet for more than a few minutes, it's short and to the point. The pastor tells us that death is not death, but rebirth into a new body in the presence of the Savior who gave his life on the cross and rose again so we might do the same. There is a scripture reading and a prayer relinquishing the body. There's a steady insistence that the real Nancy won't be buried in her satin-lined box, that the real Nancy is free. But I'm not buying it. If she's already gone, what's the point of standing out here in the rain? Why the carefully placed Astroturf and the polished brass scaffolding? The pastor remembers Nancy as cheerful, always singing. But she wasn't. She was a royal pain in the ass.

I know I shouldn't be thinking bad things about her. I picture myself inside the casket when it touches bottom. The first shovelful of mud and gravel hitting the lid with a thud. The last sliver of light disappearing. The dark complete under the weight of more and more and more soil. I swallow hard, tamping down the sick in my throat.

Grammy is holding a rose. In the silence following the

Amen, she steps forward and lays it on the coffin. Her eyes are glassy under the plastic rain bonnet protecting her curls. When the men from the funeral home begin to lower Nancy into the hole, the nausea flares into my mouth. I can't watch. Mom, Sue and I turn away.

Someone has brought lunch to the house. Chewing feels like punishment, but talking is torture. We chew and chew and lift our water glasses to our mouths, coaxing the food down our throats. Mom rests on the couch after lunch with her knees propped on cushions. The eyelid of her good eye flutters, cutting strands of tears.

We head out again to church. When we arrive, the parking lot is packed. A line of people snakes out the door and down the front walkway. A wheelchair appears at the curb for Mom. Someone must have considered how exhausting the trip would be from the car to the foyer, then from the foyer down the long corridor. Mom rides self-consciously past the stream of people waiting to sign the guest book. The sanctuary is already full when we take our seats at the front. One of the deacons and a few boys from youth group are setting up extra rows of folding chairs. Even so, some people wind up standing in back and along the side walls, holding their coats. Across the aisle from us, several rows are filled with kids from Nancy's school. Her three best friends sit together holding hands.

The service is long. It's difficult to stay focused. Tedd gives a lengthy eulogy. Our pastor gives a shorter one. Their message is basically the same. Nancy is not dead, she's been born to new life through Jesus Christ, a life every one of us can have. Three sisters we know from camp harmonize through a song we used to sing in the dining hall after meals. Both Bruce and my youth group leader get up to speak.

I don't hear what they say. My ears and throat have thickened with something dark and viscous like tar. God is watching. God is waiting for the great thing he spared me to accomplish.

The pastor announces there will be no receiving line. My parents are not well enough to greet all those in attendance. He asks the mourners instead to exit the sanctuary and line the front walk silently in a show of support. My family stays seated until the rows behind us have cleared. Mom refuses to run this gauntlet in a wheelchair. She will walk to the car on her own two feet, no matter how labored and slow. Bruce stands between Mom and Dad, linking arms. Sue and I follow behind. We take one step, then stop. Another step, then stop. The way we used to when we practiced getting married, humming the Wedding March and balancing Hardy Boys books on our heads. Outside, people are four deep along the walkway. I can tell from behind that Mom is concentrating on placing each foot. Dad is focused on the crowd, nodding to this person and that as he passes. Very much like a queen greeting her loyal subjects.

I shiver and wish again for my trench coat, the one I'll never be able to wear. It's balled up in the trash in our garage. The pastor's wife told me that on the night of the crash she was waiting outside the Emergency Room. Somehow my coat got handed to her. It was brown from all the blood it had soaked up and it stunk of gasoline. She took it to our house, filled the tub in the kids' bathroom upstairs and left it there to soak. But the stink wouldn't lift.

"Sorry," she said. "I had to throw it out."

•

MOM AND DAD SPEND the winter in their bedroom recovering. They wake up in the morning, dress, make their bed and sit on top of the covers. Propped up by piles of pillows, they read and doze. Dad is forever flexing his right wrist. He has no sensation in his fingers and blames the surgeon who reattached his hand. "My practice is ruined," he says. The patch over Mom's eye makes it difficult for her to focus on task work or the pages of a book for more than short stretches at a time. Mostly she listens to Dad complain, her one visible eye roaming.

My job is to bring them things, to do whatever Mom can't. I carry their meals upstairs on trays. At supper time, we eat together in their room, trays on our laps. I sit facing them in the rocking chair at the foot of the bed, an audience of one. They look like a pair of exiled rulers, beaten up and dumped on an island the size of a mattress. I am their sole remaining subject. I know it's my duty to serve and obey, but it's not easy.

One night after supper I am collecting the dirty dishes and stacking our trays when Dad announces that, of the three of us, he is the one who suffers most. Nancy was the first person who ever really loved him, he says.

Nobody goes into her room. Her teddy bears and Raggedy Anns sit lined up on the pine chest the way she left them.

School is my escape. I run for the bus in the early half-dark and don't return until well after the sun has set. Snow squeaks like Styrofoam as I trudge back up the dark street. Only the windows in a few upper rooms of our house are lit. I take my place in the rocker at the foot of my parents' bed and balance a supper tray on my knees. Then I retreat to my room, close the door, pull my chair up to the desk. I can't focus on my homework. I stare at my reflection in the window. I want someone to say something to me. A friend to ask how I am.

At a youth group meeting, when we draw into a circle and take turns praying out loud, I ask God to please tell Nancy that I miss her. This brings the whole group to tears, which I find intensely satisfying. They have noticed me. Now they'll have to draw close, coax me out. But when prayer time is over everyone bolts for the pizza and Coke, cutting me a wide berth.

I'm drawn to the loners in school, the ones at the fringes. I find them lurking in the art studio, smoking on the hill, eating lunch in the library. I spend hours beside them in the photography lab, moving prints from one chemical tray to the next. We cut classes together. We joy-ride to White Pond or Walden Pond with The Cars or Bob Marley on the tape deck. At the first sign of false spring, we take off our shoes and stand in the mud, sharing a clove cigarette.

I steal a note pad from Dad's desk with his name and medical credentials printed across the top. I practice forging his signature, and once I have it down I begin writing notes excusing myself from whole days of classes. I'm careful to imply each time that these absences are medically necessary. I let the receptionist in the school office imagine that I'm wrestling with mysterious injuries sustained in the plane crash. With an entire day to myself, I ride the commuter train into Boston. I poke around the shops at Faneuil Hall. I explore the produce stalls in Haymarket Square and the Italian cafes of the North End. I catch the subway to Cambridge and browse the second-hand clothing and record stores in Harvard Square.

Because we need money, and because there is so much to do to revive Dad's medical practice after their long convalescence, my parents go back to work. Mom hounds the insurance companies about overdue claims. She types billing reminders for patients who are months behind. She starts making payments on past-due rent and utilities. Dad sees patients. He frets about the regulars from before the crash who haven't rebooked their missed appointments. We meet briefly around the supper table at the end of each day. The rocking chair at the foot of their bed is now reserved for lectures and punishments. I know I'm in trouble when they summon me to that chair. Propped up in bed, Dad opens the proceedings the same way every time. "I'm going to tell you something you're not capable of understanding yet," he says. "But you need to hear it anyway."

When my final report card comes at the end of eleventh grade, my parents call me to the rocker. Dad reads a long list of dates: the excused absences I faked and the classes I cut without bothering to forge a note. He asks me if I want to end up like Bruce.

"Your brother started skipping classes in his sophomore year," Dad says. "He sat in the cafeteria all day long gorging on French fries and ice cream. Scavenging food off of other kids' plates. And you know what happened to him."

I do. He got fat. He was sent to boarding school out of state. He earned his high school diploma, but he stayed fat. If I continue cutting classes, I may or may not get sent away. But I'll definitely wind up fat.

•

DURING MY SENIOR YEAR, Mom asks me to help out in Dad's office. I can work part time after school, she suggests, and earn some extra money. I know she wants to spend time with me. Sometimes I want that, too. More often I want to escape. But I agree to put in a few hours after school to make her happy. I file medical charts and dust the waiting room and unpack vitamin shipments and sort the mail. I run errands to the post office and the pharmacy. I cover the phone and make appointments when Mom goes grocery shopping. The whole time wishing I were somewhere else.

I begin finding excuses to skip work. I stay after school for yearbook. She looks at me accusingly when I slink into the kitchen where she's fixing dinner. "You've missed three days this week," she says. To make it up to her, I set the table.

In my last semester of high school, a friend gets the recipe for Kahlua from her older sister. I dress up in church clothes, squeeze into a pair of Mom's heels, dig for the cubic zirconium in her jewelry box and slip it on my ring finger. I am so much taller than the purple-faced man behind the cash register at the liquor store he doesn't think to card me when I plunk down a jug of 90-proof vodka.

My parents head to Florida. I'm going to join them in a week, for spring break. I stay with Vi while they're gone, but I spend a lot of time alone in our house after school splitting vanilla beans, brewing gallons of coffee and dissolving a whole box of sugar. When the dark, syrupy mixture is cool, I strain it, add the vodka and dole out my concoction into empty juice bottles and peanut butter jars. On the Friday night before I am to fly down to meet my parents, I tell Vi that I'll be staying overnight at a friend's house. I go home instead, to get drunk with my friends.

The sugary liquor combined with all the other things people bring to drink and the cigars we smoke turn the place into a vomitorium. The next morning, before catching my flight, I clean the puke off the bathroom floors in a blinding hangover and drag a trash bag full of empty bottles deep into the woods. When we get home a week later, Mom finds what I missed. After I confess, she tells me that as soon as she saw me coming through the arrival gate at the airport, she knew I'd done something wrong. Something I couldn't take back. I am grounded for the rest of the school year. I consider protesting. I'm almost eighteen. The punishment seems steep, but I realize I deserve it.

I can't erase all the bad things I've done, but maybe I can make up for the trouble I've caused. Instead of applying to art colleges for the fall, I decide to apply to the Christian college Sue goes to. If I can get in, if I earn a diploma from Billy Graham's alma mater, Mom and Dad will be pleased. By the time high school graduation rolls around, I'm still on the waiting list for admission. When the acceptance letter finally arrives, my parents are excited. We'll caravan out to Chicago in August, they say, Sue and me in her car and Dad and Mom in the station wagon.

I spend the summer working at the ice cream stand down the road from our house. Sometimes Dad comes to pick me up on his motorcycle and I make him a mocha frappe. He always asks me the same two questions while I'm scooping the ice cream into the mixing cup. Question one: How about one more scoop? And question two: What's the difference between a milkshake and a frappe? After I add an extra scoop and remind him that a milkshake is flavored syrup blended with milk and a frappe is a milkshake with ice cream in it, he tells me all about the malted milkshakes he used to drink as a teenager in Philly, and how in that city a milkshake was made with ice cream, so there was no such thing as a frappe.

Dad eats his frappe with a long-handled spoon while I clean the mixers and restock the napkin dispensers and wipe the counters with bleach. Out in the parking lot, he hands me the extra helmet and I fasten the chin strap while he revs the engine. My uniform is a seafoam-green polyester dress that zips up the front. Although I've let out the hem as far as it will go, it still falls only to mid-thigh. I try not to flash my underpants while I hike my leg over the back of the motorcycle. More than once, while I'm concentrating on holding down my dress, my leg presses against the hot exhaust pipe and sticks. It sears a burn the size of a grapefruit to the inside of my calf.

In July, a friend's sister turns twenty-one and their parents let her throw a keg party in their back yard. I'm standing by the keg trying to prolong my conversation with a guy I've had a crush on since sophomore year when somebody spills beer down the front of my skirt. My friend takes me inside and helps me clean up, but I can still smell it on the drive home. I dip my head toward the skirt to see how bad it is. The station wagon swerves off the country road and side-swipes a telephone pole. I scream and keep going. At home, with the car in the garage, I creep around to the passenger side. Both door panels are bashed in. I can't keep from crying in my parents' room as I tell them the story. Dad pulls on his bathrobe and rushes down to see the damage for himself. Mom asks me, angrily, if I'm hurt. I shake my head and sob through another string of apologies.

"I know you're sorry," she says. "I'm just disgusted with you right now."

Dad takes the car to the dealership for repairs. He tells me the insurance company requires him to file an accident report. Since no police cruiser was called to the scene, I will have to go into the Concord Police Department and make a statement. To the same people who pulled me out of the plane. "They'll ask if you had any alcohol that night," he tells me, and makes it clear that if I confess to drinking beer before clipping the pole, our car insurance will go up. "But I'm not going to tell you what to say. That's your responsibility."

We sit across the desk from a uniformed officer. Even before Dad mentions the plane crash, I'm pretty sure he remembers us. The man is kind, smiling the whole time he takes my statement. He jokes about how close to the road the telephone poles are around here, especially on the rural stretch I was driving. He recalls that it might have been a little foggy, maybe even raining that night, which would have made it harder for anyone to negotiate those turns in the dark. When he asks me if I'd been drinking, his tone remains casual, like it's an afterthought. I shake my head.

Now I've lied to the people who saved my life. The ones who got me out of there before the surgeons could slice off my arm with their scalpels. The ones in uniforms stained black with gasoline and blood.

I'm free to go.

II.
THE WRONG DAUGHTER

IN HIGH SCHOOL I envisioned college as a gentle green expanse of lacrosse fields, reading arbors and Frisbee on the quad. The suburban Midwest where I land instead is a grid strung mile after mile with strip malls, parking surfaces and big box stores. I try to convince myself the complete change of scenery is what I needed anyway. Maybe in this place things will be different. Maybe I'll remember how to talk to people.

Because my roommate and I were both admitted at the last minute, there is no room for us on the girl's wing of the freshman dorm. The college assigns us to a guest room reserved for campus visitors. It's much bigger than the regular dorm suites. We have twin beds instead of bunks and our own private bathroom. But our window faces the boy's wing of the building. Several times a night somebody throws something at the glass to get my pretty roommate to open the curtains. After six weeks of this, I want out. A sophomore girl in my history class tells me her roommate is leaving and invites me to take her place. I jump at the chance.

The mood in the basement of the sophomore dorm is familiar. There are girls who don't change their clothes or leave their rooms for days, not even to go to the dining hall. They subsist on instant coffee, Cup-a-Soup and vats of air-popped corn. My new roommate stays up late making out with her boyfriend in a storage closet. One night she comes in crying. He is pressuring her to have sex. Even though he's one of the cutest guys on campus, she knows she has to break up with him. After that, we play the saddest songs from our combined record collection over and over and let clothes and books and papers pile up until we can't see out the window.

My drawing instructor pins up my work as an example of bad technique. He wanted us to blend the charcoal pencil strokes until they softened and disappeared, but I liked the effect of leaving them pronounced on the page. I decide to drop the class. I'm a photographer anyway. Drawing isn't important.

A few weeks later, my English professor hands back an essay with a note saying he wants to talk to me. I avoid him for as long as I can. When he eventually corners me after class, it is to praise my work, not to criticize it. At first I think he's mistaken me for someone else. But he knows my name. He asks me to think about changing my major to English, insisting the department would be happy to have "another fine writer." I can't remember the last time that a teacher has commended my writing. In high school, my yearbook copy needed lots of work. Mrs. Howard, the remedial writing teacher, marked up draft after draft in her slanted cursive.

I thought I was barely literate. Sue, on the other hand, is a senior English major and straight A student. That must be why my professor wants me to join his department. He thinks I'll do as well as my sister. I'm sure I'll disappoint him, but I decide to make the switch anyway. When I bring the transfer form to the art department chair to sign, he doesn't try to change my mind.

•

A THEATER MAJOR I meet in French class suggests we apply to live in the French House sophomore year. I trade one basement room for another. Ours is next to the furnace, so there's a constant smell of gas. In a hard rain, the floor becomes one giant puddle. Upstairs there is an international student from Belgium and some girls from missionary families who grew up in Africa. They converse in the kitchen at lightning speed. My roommate and I have no clue what they're saying.

I am lying on the top bunk studying a spider web I've been watching all week. My roommate comes in trailing a string of heavy sighs, each one more histrionic than the last. I lie there not talking, not asking her what's wrong. She slams some things around on her desk and finally announces, accusingly, that she's failing history. I don't tell her that things will be all right. It would take too much effort.

"Thanks so much for your concern," she snaps. I stare at the web. She kicks the rickety bed post, rocking my bunk. "You need to get up," she rages at me. "Get out of bed for a change. It's the middle of the afternoon. Do something! Stop moping around."

I tell her, quietly, eyes locked on the cobweb, that she needs to mind her own fucking business.

Chapel attendance is mandatory except on Wednesdays. There are work-study students posted in the balcony with seating charts to keep track of who shows up and who doesn't. When I haven't been to a service in a month, the dean of women calls my sister into her office. Sue relays the dean's concerns to Mom and Dad, who call me to talk about getting some counseling.

I agree to meet with the Christian social worker the dean has recommended. I always try to do what my parents ask. I want to be the pleasant, cooperative girl they raised me to be, the girl who stirs no wake. I want to fix things, meet needs, make people love me. But it feels like I've broken too many rules, cut too many ties to expect that much.

I point Sue's car straight north of campus, past the truck dealership, the high school, the chicken place, the burger place, the U-Haul, the Jewel-Osco. Peggy's office is on the right, a brick office building, not to be confused with the brick bank or the brick Methodist church. I dislike her immediately. Her smoothly coiffed hair. Her tailored tweeds and heathered sweaters. Her trim calves zipped into leather boots. She glances repeatedly from my composed face to the untouched box of Kleenex at my elbow. It's been a long time since I've cried, but I won't give her the satisfaction of unleashing my tears.

After a few sessions, she points out that I'm always wearing scarves. My favorite is a patchouli-soaked Palestinian kaffiyeh I ordered from the back of *Rolling Stone* magazine. She informs me that a scarf is a symbolic barricade between the heart and the head.

What a joke. I can't wait to tell my friends.

I don't sleep much. I take late night walks to a playground where I pump hard on a swing. The chains loosen for an instant at the top of each arc, then jerk me backwards into the descent. When there are stars, I pick a point between two and aim my feet there, willing myself to disappear. When I doze, I dream some variation of the same thing: I'm being chased through a dark house. Sometimes in the dream I find the door and escape, but when I run into the street I am hit by a car, the warm metallic taste of blood rising in my mouth.

I lose track of my parts, gone numb for days at a time. I can't taste. I can't hear birds or footsteps or my own breath. Other days my ears ring and a shrill panic knifes high in my chest. Instead of studying, which doesn't hold my focus for more than a few minutes at a time, I hide in the music library, where Sue used to work part-time shelving albums. Listening to LPs through a foam headset, I invent romantic fantasies or plot revenge against people who are glossy and healthy and whose skin isn't so tightly stretched across their skulls.

Peggy announces that I am mildly schizophrenic. She doesn't explain what this means. Instead, she sends me off for winter break with an assignment. I am to gather my family for a candid conversation about the airplane crash. Everyone should be encouraged to share their feelings about what happened. She recommends enlisting a family friend or pastor to act as moderator. I tell her that, as a rule, New England Yankees, we descendants of Puritans, tend not to share our feelings. But Peggy has faith in us. She believes if we come together, we'll find a way to open up. God will guide us to unburden ourselves. Although I am skeptical, this scenario is tantalizing. I imagine being pulled again from the carcass of the airplane, this time into the embrace of my family.

On the day of the big meeting, we gather in the living room. My brother Tedd has come to guide the discussion. We arrange ourselves on the sofa and chairs with plenty of space between us. There's a prayer to start us off, requesting God's blessing on the proceedings. Dad talks first but I don't hear what he's saying. I'm too nervous waiting for my turn. When it comes, I have just one thing to say to him.

"I know you wish Nancy was the one who lived instead of me."

Dad bows his head. Tears begin to drop into his lap. He reaches for the pressed handkerchief in his back pocket. Mom jumps up to comfort him. When he speaks, it's to say that Nancy's death is still too much to bear. Sometimes he wants to die himself. He reminds us how much harder all of this has been on him. Finally he admits it. If he'd been given the choice, I would be the one who died. He doesn't look up. He doesn't say, forgive me for feeling this way. He doesn't say, but you're still my daughter. He doesn't say, it's good you're alive. He clutches the handkerchief.

There won't be any more sessions with Peggy. I already knew what Dad was thinking, but I didn't need to hear him say it in front of everyone. If that's the kind of help I'm going to get from therapy, I can definitely live without it.

Like everyone else at my college, I signed a pledge not to drink or smoke or use drugs or dance or gamble or attend R-rated movies. Even though it's grounds for instant dismissal, I dump a beer into a Styrofoam cup before leaving for class in the morning. I go back for refills during the day, sipping my way across campus through a straw. When a source with something more potent shows up, I take to snorting lines of coke and staying awake for days at a time. To crash, I drink jug wine and smoke some pot. After each of these binges, I swear I'll never do it again.

I am interested in having sex. And ashamed of my life-long failure at finding a boyfriend. The closest I've come was in high school, when I made out a couple of times with a hockey player in the back seat of a friend's car. I've never been on a real date. I wonder if I'm even capable of coupling the way normal people do. The guys I get interested in tend to be the ones people spread rumors about. The ones, they say, who slip out after midnight to meet other guys under the bleachers.

Men flock to my friend Kristyn. Boyfriends, friends of boyfriends, strangers. Even her dad flies out to Chicago for periodic visits during the semester. She's not a flirt. She treats everyone the same, like we all have interesting or important things to say. I study the way she moves through a day like there were no impediments, no roadblocks to slow her down. When I suggest we should go live in Paris after graduation, she doesn't just agree it would be cool. She figures out how to make it happen.

•

OUR STUDIO APARTMENT IN the Latin Quarter is dark and stinks of mildew. There is a heavy brown armoire, matching bunk beds and manure-brown carpeting. When the flocked wallpaper starts peeling off in sheets, Kristyn persuades the landlord to let us whitewash the sweating walls. One enormous window opens onto the interior courtyard, where we track the comings and goings of the other tenants. There is the former circus performer who throws dinner parties for acrobats and opera singers. They drink and argue late into the night. There is the couple upstairs who snipe at one another each morning until the man leaves for work in his shiny suit. When he gets home, they pick up where they left off. Our next-door neighbor is a Canadian hairstylist who fled an Indian reservation on the Hudson Bay for the constant fashion shoot of Paris. Our two apartments share a wall. He keeps his radio tuned to a club music station, cranks up the volume and claps and snaps to the beat, sometimes letting out a whoop-whoop.

We both find waitressing jobs and boyfriends. The guy Kristyn meets is a tall Frenchman, and very kind. He surprises her with a candlelit dinner he serves after hours in his parents' café. He shoots black and white photographs of her sleeping or reading and prints them in his darkroom. He assembles a decadent picnic and takes her on a day trip to the forest at Fontainebleau.

My boyfriend is actually a boy, a transplanted Brit three years younger than I am. I meet him at the American restaurant where I work. Everything about the place, from the menu to the décor, baffles the French. The men's bathroom is labeled Elton John and the women's is Olivia Newton John. The pizza is served in a cake pan. The cakes are made with carrots. The wine is from California. Trendy French couples who wander in tend not to return. The regulars are native English speakers. There are Marines from the American embassy who scarf down trays of deep-dish sausage pizza and pitchers of beer, and Brits who never make it past the bar. At closing time I head out with the girls to a Tex-Mex place around the corner where we spend our tip money on tequila sunrises. The Brits follow and order more pints. When the Marines show up, the night ends in a fist fight, tumbling Wild-West style into the street.

At first I resist the most likable of the Brits because he's too young for me. He's determined, however, and knows how to be adorable. One night at closing I dash to catch the last Metro and he chases after me, both of us sprinting down the Champs-Élysées beneath a soft rain. The tourists lined up outside the Lido watch as he grabs my arm and I spin to face him. "Kiss me!" he demands. "Why won't you kiss me?" He pursues me through the rain several nights that week until he wins me over.

Painful as it is, I do not bleed the first time we have sex. Or the second, or the third. Throughout our first weeks together he alternates between calling me Beauty and calling me a liar. One Sunday morning at his parents' house he sneaks me into his room from my place on the landing, where his mother set up my cot. He's inside of me immediately, not bothering to lift the T-shirt I've been sleeping in. He thrusts hard and high and urgently, and then just as urgently my blood comes down. He doesn't notice until after he has come. The back of my T-shirt is soaked and clinging to my ass. I send him to rummage for some pads or tampons in his mother's bathroom while she's downstairs in the kitchen trussing a roast. He is rattled by the sudden rush of blood from between my legs. He brings me an assortment of scavenged supplies, holding them away from his body, and bolts downstairs for tea and homemade scones while I clean up.

According to my boyfriend, to order a proper serving of beer in France you have to ask for *un formidable*. If you say beer or draft you get a half pint, often in a feminine-looking glass. Fine, maybe, for birds and poofs, but unacceptable to any subject of the Queen who takes his drink seriously.

I discover soon enough that my boyfriend cannot be enticed from the bar on any night of the week for almost any reason, even with all of Paris beckoning. We manage to see a couple of movies together, but only in the neighborhoods where familiar groups of drinkers congregate in familiar bars. On these nights he orders two pints at a time to make up for his late start. We argue more and more frequently, and eventually he hits me. Once that seal is broken, it's easy to let it happen again. The morning after, he is always tender and remorseful, mortified that he could have done such a thing. He tucks a love note between the pages of the book I'm reading, or leaves an Asterix cartoon folded under my pillow. I accept his apology every time. I apologize back for provoking him. Often, during make-up sex, he can't help calling attention to one part of my body or another and cataloging its faults. When I am on my hands and knees, for example, he is preoccupied with the way my naked belly hangs toward the floor, flapping helplessly with each thrust. Look how fat you are, he tells me. I look, and I see.

On a weekend when his father is away for business, he convinces his mother to let him throw a party. She misses her social set from Coventry and the Saturday nights when they used to roll up the sitting room carpet to dance. She agrees a party would liven up the place. A girl no one seems to know turns up late, mixed in with a fresh group of revelers. I watch as she deflects the advances of some of the older guys and edges close to my boyfriend. She is British too, with soft-looking brown hair and distracting tits. They talk about music. She hates American bands. He agrees. "A bunch of pricks and prats," he says, nodding. He tells me I look tired and shoos me upstairs. "She doesn't fancy parties, that one," I hear him complain as I retreat. At the top of the stairs, I turn to watch him slide his hands beneath the girl's sweater while his dog shits on the floor in a dark corner.

I have missed the last train and can't afford a taxi, even if I could convince one to venture this far out of Paris in the middle of the night. I take a long shower. I dress. I stuff a pile of cassettes that belong to me into a plastic bag and sit down on the cot, coat folded in my lap, to wait for the trains to begin running again. The house is quiet when I slip downstairs in the five o'clock dark. I pick my way over snoring bodies face down on the sitting room floor. My boyfriend and the girl with the tits are among them, passed out in a single sleeping bag.

I am unlatching the front door when someone steps up behind me. "Wait," a voice whispers, "I'm coming with you." It's the oldest lad in the gang. Somewhere in his thirties, dark and slight of build, he's not as boisterous as the others, and he has a grown-up job. He tells me he needs to get home. We walk to the train station in the dark. He buys both tickets. He pats my hand as we ride the empty train into Paris.

"Bloody cheek," he says, shaking his head. "If I had someone like you! Let's just say you wouldn't catch me pulling a stunt like that."

He hails a cab outside Saint-Lazare station and asks me to come along for a good English breakfast. Then he'll give me a lift home. I'm not hungry. I'm not thirsty. I'm not angry. I'm not sleepy. I'm scooped out. I go along because it's too much trouble to do anything else.

After breakfast we walk to the residence hotel where he keeps his car in the garage. He wants to fetch something from his room first. Cigarettes or car keys. I follow him up. He closes the door and invites me to sit while he rummages through a drawer. There are no chairs, so I perch on the edge of the bed. He moves quickly. His grip is startlingly strong. He presses his mouth against mine and leans into me, forcing me onto my back. I see myself lying there, very still, while his thin lips and small hands scuttle over my body. I leave the bed and drift out the window, down the Avenue de l'Opera, over the courtyards of the Louvre, following the quai along the river toward home. Then I'm back again, stuffed into my skin, the handles of the plastic bag I've lugged all this way biting into my wrist. I am bigger than he is. I throw him off and stand up. Four strides get me out the door.

On the bottom bunk in my dark apartment with the window shuttered, I count the number of times the phone rings before the caller hangs up and redials. I unplug the jack. I dissolve some sleeping tablets in a glass of water. They fizz. When I'm able to roust myself from bed, I pack and fly home to Boston. The first few nights, Mom rubs my back to help me fall asleep. When I doze, I jolt awake in a panic, unsure of where I am. Or I sleepwalk. One night I wake up standing in the spare bedroom where Dad's up reading.

"You'd better watch your step," he warns me. "You think sex is a kick, but you'll keep paying the price. There are more productive ways to spend your time."

I leave home again for Chicago, to be among friends who moved into the city after college. I string together part-time work and save for a return ticket to Paris. It's still the place in the world where I most want to be.

•

MY SECOND PARISIAN BOYFRIEND is from Nice, an Anglophile working on a graduate degree in translation. His previous girlfriend was Canadian. They lived and studied together in the south of France. He saw her alive for the last time on February fourteenth. Before she left for school on the Vespa, he didn't tell her that he loved her. He had planned a surprise dinner for Valentine's Day and didn't want her to catch on. She was hit and killed in traffic on the way to campus.

He tips my face to his in the Metro and kisses me.

"I like you a lot, OK?" he says. And then, "I don't like the Metro. It smells like death."

It's been more than two years since his girlfriend was killed, more than two years since their last kiss. He is reluctant to have sex, not certain he's ready. When we spend the night together, he enters me but doesn't ejaculate. At least not while he's awake. Much later, from the depths of his dreaming, he reaches for me like a starving man and says, "I love you." When he comes, he calls her name.

He stops dropping by the apartment after class. He stops phoning. I wait. One night I am up reading in bed, waiting. I fall asleep and dream that I am striking a match. I toss it beneath the covers and they ignite with a popping sound, like gas jets. The bed around me jumps into flame. I throw the covers off and wake up diving to the floor. I lie there studying the ceiling, steadying my heartbeat, still waiting for his footfalls in the courtyard. Then I drink some wine, turn out the lights and crawl back into bed. When I can't wait any longer, I trek past the Arc de Triomphe to the manicured edge of the city where he rents a maid's room, no kitchen, no shower, toilet in the hall. Up six flights to the top of his building. He is angry that I have come. He won't say why he has stopped calling. Why he has chosen the dead girl over the living one.

"Comme ça," he shrugs.

After this, winter comes. I spend it alone, sleeping whenever I'm not at work teaching English to housewives and teenagers. When sleep won't come, I lie in bed smoking, watching gray rain fall from gray sky onto gray angles of rain-oiled buildings.

For at least my first year in France, I recoiled from the phone whenever it rang for fear of not understanding the person on the other end of the line, or of not being able to make the right words come out of my mouth in reply. Now in the dank, changeless months of winter, when the phone rings I'm afraid I'll have to invent one more excuse not to get together with another concerned friend. Eventually, they stop calling. Eventually, the wind blusters up and blows spring across bridges, down boulevards, through my window. I begin to walk when the days brighten and coatless afternoons are tinged with a different quality of melancholy. The soft sadness of standing on a bridge alone as a river barge passes beneath.

I walk and walk and walk, past impromptu tango lessons on the quai and pick-up soccer games in the grassy median between boulevards. Past dog walkers gossiping and flower vendors setting out pails of narcissus and iris. Past Africans in acid-green jumpsuits sweeping water through the gutters. I cover miles of spring each day, and in these miles my plan takes shape. I will prove to myself once and for all that it is possible—that it is preferable—to have sex without falling in love. During the summer that follows, my last in Paris before returning to the States for graduate school, I have no difficulty recruiting guys willing to help execute my plan. The ones I pick for the job have nothing in common but this: to a man, they don't love me.

•

I EXPECT A BLEAK industrial city, but Milwaukee in summer

is green against the blue edge of Lake Michigan. After the first meeting of my first graduate seminar, I go out for coffee with a woman from Louisiana. She wants to hear about Paris. I tell her I'd only planned to stay a year, since I'd been accepted to the creative writing program, but the university kept letting me defer enrollment, and Paris was so great it was hard to leave. A man happens by our table and, because grad students from his department hang out with grad students from ours, he sits down. He has an Italian name. Eventually the table fills up with names in other languages, like Irish and Hindi. It feels right to be a student again, among these unlikely names in this unlikely city. It will be good to focus on my course work, and sometimes go for coffee after class to continue the discussion, and not get sidetracked by ridiculous plans like proving myself impervious to love.

By Halloween, the man with the Italian name and I have become a couple. Falling for him is different from the way I have fallen before. I don't lie awake at night thinking about him. I don't lose my appetite. I interpret these as signs of a connection based on something more mature and abiding than lust. He invites me to a movie he's already seen just so he can sit beside me for two hours in the dark, reading subtitles and brushing elbows. I drive up behind him in traffic and exclaim, "There he is!" He saves a message I leave on his answering machine to play over and over and over. I take frequent walks past the places I've run into him by chance. He brings me a lock of his hair in response to a poem I've written about Samson.

The first time we make out, it takes me by surprise when

he cuts our kissing short. "Can't we just fuck?" he asks. I do not tell him that I'd like to be kissed some more, and touched and undressed, first slowly, then with urgency. Instead, I excuse myself and head to the bathroom to insert my diaphragm. Our sex is frequent and not particularly lingering. It feels good while it lasts, the weight of him settling over me, muscled and tightly wound. His whole body spasms when he comes, a succession of violent shakes. I want to hold on, to feel his quaking again and again. I don't come myself. I never have, with any of my boyfriends. I don't think about how to change this. I wouldn't know what to ask of a man.

We laugh a great deal. We drink a great deal. In our first few months as a couple, more than once he becomes a jealous drunk. There is no violence when he accuses me of liking the guy who I said hello to at the bar or sat next to in class. Instead, his jealousy is lugubrious. I am untrustworthy because he is unlovable. Why would I want him anyway, he wonders aloud, slumped on the musty carpet in my apartment. This is a question I understand the way I understand breathing. It's the common thread stitching our stories together. It makes me want to take care of him, to wrap us both in stronger, surer arms.

Like me, he has a complicated family history. He was born in Milan, in a clinic beside the church where Leonardo painted "The Last Supper." His mother was a college student. His father was a German tourist she'd met at the beach and had sex with a couple of times. Her first pregnancy test came back negative. Not until she was five months along did she realize there had been an error. When she was told that the Italian state would not legally recognize her child unless he bore his father's name, she boarded a train for Germany. In exchange for their surname, the man's family demanded she relinquish all filial and financial claims.

When her water broke, a cousin took her to the clinic. Her mother stayed home making secret arrangements for the baby to be adopted immediately. She was counting on the element of surprise and hoping her daughter would be too weak to protest. The cousin foiled these plans, demanding that the newborn be placed instead with a guardian until his mother could finish her studies.

When he was ten days old, my boyfriend was taken to the countryside and placed in the care of a stranger. A farmer and his wife raised him alongside their own young children. He was three when his mother returned for him. She had met an American who offered to marry her so that she could emigrate to the United States. The boy moved away with her although he had little notion of who she was. In Colorado he pedaled a tricycle around in a circle and cried for his mother, the farmer's wife who had nursed him. He did not understand that the woman who'd brought him to the mountains in an airplane was actually his mother. He stopped responding when she spoke to him. After weeks of silence, he began to talk again, but only in English.

His mother scraped up teaching work and took him along as she moved from one university gig to the next. They left the American man behind. It was just the two of them now, crossing the western states in a Mustang. Once, in California, when he was five, he woke up afraid and padded through the apartment looking for her, but she'd gone out. He found the faculty phone directory and dialed his way through the list, asking for his mother. In another college town he remembered a man with a motorcycle who sometimes yelled in the kitchen. She yelled back. Plates were smashed. One summer his mother tried to quit smoking and finish her doctoral dissertation all at the same time. He crawled out the bedroom window every morning and stayed away until nightfall to escape her moods.

His third grade teacher made fun of his name, Matteo, so he changed it to the clipped American version, lopping off the soft vowel ending. When I meet him twenty years later he has only just learned the story of his German father and reclaimed his Italian name in some social circles. At work and on legal documents he continues to use his American name. We joke about how he could exploit this dual identity. He could be a spy. He could have a secret life.

After six months as a couple, we decide to look for our own apartment. When we announce that we're moving in together, the friend who introduced us takes me aside. The two of them had briefly been an item. They'd taken a road trip together to New Orleans where they stayed with her sister, a child psychiatrist. During the visit, her sister came to suspect that he was probably incapable of forming adult attachments. His confusing childhood, with its ruptured bonds, would shadow him throughout his life. Healthy adult relationships would be a stretch. This was enough for my friend to call it off. I thank her for these insights and for her concern, even as I consign her prognosis to the rubbish heap. His story is what draws me to him. It makes me feel necessary. It intersects with mine in ways that are achingly familiar. It gives me purpose. I want to minister to his needs, to ease his pain.

Still, I'm nervous about telling Mom and Dad that we've decided to live together. They will not approve, because the church does not approve. When I call them to break the news, Mom wants me to know that, although she is disappointed in me, she will not let this breach of values come between us. Dad takes the receiver to tell me that any man who lets me smoke doesn't really love me, so I must have chosen poorly.

But I'm sure he's the right choice for me. His is the best, most tender love I've known from a man. Mom shocked me once by saying that a woman can tell she's truly in love when she would eat a man's shit if she had to. It was the only time I ever heard her curse. Now I get it. I would do anything for him.

We never fight. We rarely even disagree. We have almost identical tastes in most things: movies, food, music, places to travel, people to vote for, which art we would buy if we could and which we'd just look at, what jokes are funny and what jokes aren't. We throw dance parties and dinner parties. We take spontaneous day trips and researched road trips. We stay up late and sleep until midday whenever we can, breakfasting on cigarettes and shots of espresso. Lovemaking tapers off gradually during our first few years. By the time I finish my Ph.D. coursework and we leave Milwaukee for Chicago, we're having perfunctory sex maybe once a month. Monthly dwindles to never, but neither of us brings it up. Some nights I lie in bed rank with desire, listening to his steady breath, willing him to wake and reach for me. Other nights I promise myself: This is it. Tonight something will happen. But I cannot make myself act. In the daylight, we remain the easiest of companions, beyond conflict.

•

I SPEND THE YEARS in Chicago first as a lecturer, then as an adjunct professor, and finally as a visiting assistant professor of English. All part-time gigs. I was supposed to be able to make a living from teaching. But every year I apply for dozens of tenure-track jobs, getting one or two interviews and no solid offers. Each year more and more newly-minted Ph.D.s crowd me out of the academic job market. I continue to scrape together a teaching salary that amounts to little more than lunch money.

When we first lived together, the fact that I didn't earn much didn't matter to Matteo. He had a good job and was happy to share. He even invented a parable to reassure me. There once was a lazy squirrel, he said, who stayed put in the squirrel tree throughout the fall while his industrious squirrel friends and family ran around gathering acorns to store for the winter. When snow covered the ground and cold chased them back into their tree, they had plenty of food but nothing to stave off the boredom that set in. That's when the lazy squirrel revealed what he'd been up to. While the others were busy in the sunshine, he'd stayed at his desk writing stories. Stories to help pass the time while they all waited for spring. Stories that transported them to warm, fascinating, faraway places.

I am the lazy squirrel in our relationship, the creative one whose musings are underwritten by the industrious one. As the winters tick by, this arrangement loses its charm. He gets tired of being the breadwinner and the bank. He progresses from one technology job to the next, climbing the corporate ladder. My meager earnings from teaching are no match for his steadily increasing salary. He owns the condo, the car, the furniture. I can barely cover groceries and the utility bills.

After five years of part-time teaching and full-time applying for jobs, I give up on my academic career. It's time to look elsewhere. To strike out along another path. But which one? Where? I register with a temp agency and pick up clerical work in the office towers of the Chicago Loop. A week into covering for an executive assistant, the agency pulls me off the job. I lack the wardrobe and the necessary decorum. I'm not cut out to be a secretary. I can't even do that.

I'm sick of the Midwest. It's flat and the cities are too clean and I miss the ocean. I broach the topic of a move. It turns out he's been thinking along the same lines. We narrow our choices to Europe or San Francisco. He works his contacts. Silicon Valley, booming furiously, beckons. He accepts a position at a technology start-up and talks a great deal about stock options. He tells me for the first time in twelve years that I need to earn more. I can hardly wait to get to California to prove that I can squirrel money away, too. I'll rake it in. We'll live under a mountain of cash and he'll be happy with me. We hold a yard sale and hire movers. The night before they arrive to take away our possessions, we watch a rerun of "The Streets of San Francisco" on the portable TV while taping boxes.

Driving cross-country on Interstate 80, I am impatient to leave the Plains states behind and linger among the dry hills of the West. At the end of our first day on the road, we detour off the highway for dinner, then continue another 150 miles to our motel. It's after eleven when we arrive to check in and I realize I no longer have my purse. We search the car. I try to reconstruct our exit from the restaurant. I remember putting on a sweater in the parking lot before we left. Did I set my purse on the roof of the car while I did that? Is it sitting back there on the pavement in the dark? The fact that I've left something critical behind, that I've done something careless, which I never allow myself to do, makes me sick to my stomach. Then I remember the envelope of cash—several hundred dollars from our yard sale—tucked in next to my wallet. My face burns, slick with shame.

Matteo decides he will drive back to the restaurant and search the parking lot. I say that I'll go instead, and then it occurs to me that my driver's license is in the purse. As he's leaving, he tells me I should try to sleep. I sit up with the Weather Channel on mute. I call directory assistance to get the phone numbers for the restaurant and the police department. I let the restaurant phone ring thirty times before hanging up. The policeman who answers the phone in Grand Island, Nebraska after midnight is cordial but unhelpful when I ask him to check for my purse in the parking lot.

"Sorry ma'am," he says. "We can't just drive over there and look for it. It's Friday night. We're busy."

I picture the long stretch of empty prairie between the highway and the restaurant and wonder what busy means in a place where bison outnumber people.

I watch the local weather report, drink a glass of chlorinated motel water and climb into bed with the phone to cancel my credit cards. I doze, waking each time headlights on the highway sweep the room. He returns at four in the morning without the purse. We draw the black-out shades and he sleeps immediately. I call the restaurant before it opens in the morning and reach someone working in the bakery. I describe to her where we sat, near the salad bar. She sets down the receiver and is gone a long time. When she picks up the phone again she has the purse. It was hanging on the back of the chair I sat in. I break into a sweat and can't stop thanking her. We discuss the logistics of mailing the purse to our destination. But while I'm giving her the address, he wakes up enough to growl, no, we're going back. We retrace the 150 miles in silence. The woman who found my purse is behind the bakery counter. I offer her a few twenties from the untouched envelope of cash but she waves them off.

Retrieving the money feels triumphant. I cross the parking lot with the purse clutched over my head like a trophy, vowing to win many more—each one bigger and fatter—in California. I open the driver's side door and wait for him to shift over. Then I steer us across Nebraska one final time in the rain. He sleeps until Wyoming, where the sun muscles its way through the clouds.

•

WE ARRIVE IN SAN Francisco in mid-June. It turns out that

my first full-time job there is finding a place for us to live. He commutes to Sunnyvale while I scour the papers and message boards for leads on our next house-sitting gig or in-law unit. We hop from one short-term rental to another while competing with hundreds of other apartment hunters for a place to settle. Finally he gets fed up and decides we should buy something. Since all the money for the down payment on the house is his, he does not include my name on the title. Movers arrive to unload our stuff six months after we packed it in Chicago.

Through a friend of a friend, I pick up freelance copywriting assignments for technology clients. The compensation is astronomical compared to teaching, and my work earns high praise. But a loop in my head keeps accusing me of being a fraud. What do I know about databases, downtime, software cost analysis? And then the dot-com bubble bursts. People are laid off by the thousands. The newspaper reports that the number of U-Hauls leaving San Francisco has surpassed the number coming in for the first time in a decade. Commute traffic eases on the freeways. Cars move freely across the Golden Gate Bridge and the Bay Bridge and the Richmond Bridge and the Dumbarton Bridge. Miraculously, Matteo does not lose his job. But all of the air has gone out of my freelance balloon. I can't think of what in the world I'll do now to prove my worth.

I do nothing. Even this feels like work. Preparing myself for his return from the office. Getting dressed. Making dinner. Trying to fabricate a fascinating anecdote from another empty day. The move across the country was supposed to re-energize me, propel me to action. Instead, it has exhausted my ingenuity. In California, where it seems anyone can do anything she puts her mind to, I can't even decide which afternoon talk show to watch. Unfinished writing projects are no motivation. Neglecting them another week, another six months, another year won't make a difference. In the story of my life, the important events, the things that make me interesting, have already happened. The plane crash, living in Paris, meeting Matteo, getting my Ph.D., moving to California. All the juice has been wrung from the plot. There will be no more twists or epiphanies. I am thirty-nine years old and all that's left is a long, slow slide to the end. I draw the curtains for an afternoon nap.

One night very late I can't fall asleep. He hasn't come to bed yet. A friend from Chicago is staying in the guest room downstairs. Sometimes the two of them stand out on the back deck smoking and talking in the dark. I decide to go down and break it up. I need my bedmate beside me, to settle me. At the bottom of the stairs, I hear our friend moving around in his room, getting ready for bed. I hear Matteo outside talking. I can't imagine who he's talking to. As I approach the open door, I realize he's on the phone. I listen for a few moments in the dark. Then I step out onto the deck. He sees me, turns his back, tells the person on the other end of the line that he has to go.

I bolt back upstairs, hand clamped over my mouth. I dive under the covers and clutch into a fetal position, holding back the sick and the sobs. He trudges up slowly. Sits heavily on his side of the bed. He tells me it's not what I think it is. But my hamster wheel is already spinning, putting the pieces together. The whispered phone conversations at the far edge of the yard. The weekend drives he takes without me. He tells me the woman on the phone is a colleague. Someone who reminds him of me, back when we first met. They've been having drinks after work, just to talk. To compare notes on their troubled relationships. He tells me he's not having an affair, but confesses that he doesn't feel attracted to me anymore. He says he's been thinking a lot about leaving. It astonishes me that this comes as a surprise. Because it's exactly what I deserve.

In the morning, he tells me he's been in therapy for a few weeks. His therapist advised him not to end our relationship before figuring out what's gone wrong between us. He wants me to see a therapist, too. Until now, every time I've thought about getting some help, the memory of Peggy and our family conference has stopped me cold. I swore I would never go back. Now I realize I'll do anything he asks. Anything to make him change his mind. Anything to keep him here. Even that.

III.
SPOKEN BIRDS

I QUIETLY POLL FRIENDS and come up with the names of a few San Francisco therapists. I book getting-to-know-you appointments with the two whose voices I like best over the phone. One woman has a Ph.D. and a smooth-as-glass veneer. The other is a clinical social worker whose energy beams like bars of light through the slats of her chair. I choose her because she is so completely different from me, and because her light is tantalizing. I can't imagine I'll ever find my way to that kind of radiance, though. There is something huge blocking the road, spilling off the shoulder in either direction like a yeasty mountain of dough. I can't see the far edges to get a sense of its size. I don't know how to begin to dislodge it. It's like tackling a gigantic marshmallow. Sometimes I'm able to pry up a soft edge, wedge my shoulder against its bulk and push. But the mountain just spreads wider across my path. There is no budging it.

Beneath the high ceiling of a drafty Victorian, I assure Connie Rubiano that the crisis in my relationship and this mountain blocking my progress have nothing to do with the past. When we spoke on the phone, I mentioned the plane crash. I didn't come here to get sidetracked by a bunch of old business, though. My therapy needs to address the present. To fix what's wrong with me right now. To keep Matteo from leaving.

"I'd like to try and help," Connie nods. "Tell me a little more about yourself. Where are you from?"

I skip the preliminaries and jump straight to my last experience with therapy, to Peggy's diagnosis of mild schizophrenia. Connie bursts out laughing and tells me that's like declaring someone mildly pregnant. "Either you are or you aren't," she says. "And you definitely aren't."

I let out a breath I didn't realize I'd been holding since college.

"I'm from Maine, originally," I tell her, wading in.

My father was a doctor. My mother was his secretary before they got married. He was twenty years older than she was, a widower with two sons from his first marriage: my half-brothers Tedd and Allon. My mother and father had three kids together before I came along. Bruce and Sue were fine, but Wayne, the third one, died the day he was born. They cut his umbilical cord, cleared his mouth, wrapped him in a blue blanket and whisked him away. My father wouldn't let my mother see the body. They buried him in a tiny casket. She keeps his birth certificate in a box on the top shelf of her closet. Had he lived, he would have been two years older than me. Or I wouldn't have been born at all.

"Are your parents still in Maine?" Connie asks.

My father died when I was six. Mom remarried a month before my eighth birthday. We moved to Massachusetts in the middle of second grade. Just like that, we got a new house, new school, new father and a new little sister, Nancy. She was Dad's adopted daughter from a previous marriage. I've heard that story so many times I could tell it backwards. Dad and his other wife couldn't have kids of their own. Nancy's birth mother was an athlete who gave up the baby to compete in the Olympics. As a doctor with hospital privileges, Dad scrubbed in and assisted in the delivery room. The adoption agency let him take Nancy home a few days later. But his wife didn't know how to care for children. She scalded Nancy's skin under the tap and stuck her with diaper pins if she fussed on the changing table. Once when the three of them were eating dinner together, Nancy coughed. She was two years old. She failed to cover her mouth, so Dad's wife slapped her hard enough to raise finger marks on her cheek. She tore Nancy out of the high chair, stormed upstairs and dumped her in the crib.

When she wasn't torturing the baby, Dad says his wife was luring men from church over to the house and rolling around with them on a dirty mattress in the attic. In the end, she ran off with a neighbor's husband. They backed a moving van down the driveway and stole everything. Dad came home from work one night to a house emptied of furniture, clothes, books, paintings, rugs, dishes. No towels on the racks. No food in the cupboards. No water bowls for the dogs. Then the phone rang. It was the sitter calling to say Nancy was still with her. No one had come to pick her up.

"So it was your stepfather who was flying the plane that crashed?" Connie asks.

He's not my stepfather. He adopted Bruce and Sue and me,

which technically makes him our father, too. He and Mom got married as soon as his divorce was final. Right after we moved our furniture into his house, the custody battle for Nancy began. Mom and Dad left for the courthouse every morning, and every afternoon they came home worn out and on edge. At supper one night, Mom told Bruce and Sue and me that the judge wanted to talk with us the next day. I nearly peed my pants. I imagined the nasty lady who slapped baby Nancy threatening me across the aisle with the sharpened point of a diaper pin. I imagined the judge scolding me for laughing when Nancy cursed under her breath, the way she'd heard some adults do.

On the second story of the courthouse, the heels of my good shoes hammered polished tiles. The center of the building was open, a huge hole ringed by a thick railing. You could hold onto the railing and look up into a domed ceiling, or down at the people rushing in and out of the main doors on the floor below. Suspended over the opening was the biggest American flag I'd ever seen. Big enough to cover our whole house. We kids were supposed to sit still on a wooden bench outside the courtroom, but I kept asking permission to tip-toe over to the railing for another look. I wanted badly to stretch my arm through the spindles to touch the flag, but I kept my hands to myself. Counting first the red stripes, then the white stripes, then each star the size of my face, helped me worry a little less about the judge.

At times we heard angry shouts from the courtroom. When the doors finally opened, some people I didn't recognize burst out as if pushed from behind. Dad appeared and sat down next to Mom. He said it was our turn to go in. When we got up, Mom stayed seated. She wasn't coming with us. We were on our own.

The courtroom was empty, except for the judge sitting behind a tall desk at the far end. He motioned us forward. We made our way down the aisle, pressed close to one another. We stopped at the foot of the big desk and looked up. He smiled and thanked us for coming in to see him. He didn't seem angry at all. He explained that he just wanted a few minutes to talk to the three of us without any grown-ups around. How did we like our new town and our new family, he wanted to know. Did we have any pets? How about a basketball hoop? We told him about the new puppy we'd be getting when school let out, and about the neighbor kids our very same ages up and down the street, and the red tractor Dad parked in the barn behind the house, the one he'd been riding the first time Mom brought us to visit him at home. The judge listened. Then he told us Dad wanted to adopt us. He would be our new father. We would be just like his own kids. We'd even get new birth certificates to prove it, and a new last name.

"How does that sound?" the judge asked.

I didn't know what I was supposed to say. It didn't seem like we needed a new last name, but Bruce and Sue nodded their heads, so I nodded, too.

•

WHAT I LIKE ABOUT Connie is that she doesn't disguise her reactions. "Oh no!" she'll exclaim, or "You're kidding!" She's not one to feign neutrality. I can tell she is on my side. When she chimes in with a question, it's because she's concentrating on getting the story straight. I am anxious to address the problem at hand, but so is she, I realize. This is her way of getting us there.

"So your second father, who adopted you, had previously adopted another girl. She's the one who died in the plane. Do I have that right?"

I nod. "She was four years younger than me."

"What was that like, all of a sudden having a younger sister around?"

"We didn't get along," I confess. "It was a lot of responsibility."

After Dad won custody of Nancy, he took Bruce and Sue and me aside. He told us that his ex-wife might try to kidnap our new little sister and hold her for ransom. We should be on the lookout for a black VW bug, he warned. We'd already noticed a car like that cruising up our street. We told him what we'd seen and his voice got mean, as if we'd done something wrong. If we ever saw that black car again, he hissed, we were to grab Nancy and run as fast as we could into the house and lock all the doors.

"Understand?" he growled. This was Nancy's life we were talking about.

The next time the black bug came crawling by, we froze for a moment in terror. Then we dropped our bikes in the driveway and converged on Nancy. We each grabbed a limb and carried her fast over the blacktop and the grass. Sue and I slammed and locked the back door while Bruce ran to bolt the front. When Mom came in later through the garage, hauling grocery bags, she found the four of us huddled on the floor in the family room. Nancy asked tearfully if the lady in the black car had stolen her bike. "Call the police," she bawled. "Make her give it back!"

Dad always acted like she was fragile, vulnerable. I saw a different side of her. The first time she and I met was at Uncle Claude and Aunt Forrestine's house. They weren't really my aunt and uncle. They were friends who visited a lot after my first father died, before Mom married Dad. They liked to take us to the beach in their blue station wagon. Forrestine wore a bathing cap covered with tear-shaped petals and a bathing suit with a white skirt. Claude would stand chin-deep in the cold water and slide Forrestine onto his shoulders. Then he'd duck all the way under while Sue climbed onto Forrestine's shoulders. When Claude stood up, the three of them made a human tower with Sue at the top holding her nose.

I was seven and Nancy was three when her dad brought her to Uncle Claude's for dinner. Her dad would be my dad soon, but I didn't know that. After we ate, I asked to be excused. Nancy and I went out front to play. Right away, she challenged me to a contest. A half-flight of concrete steps led to Claude and Forrestine's door. Nancy wanted to see who could jump up the most steps. She leapt to the first one, so I did too. It was easy. I was tall for my age, with long legs. She sprang back to the sidewalk and gritted her teeth, intent on jumping up two. She barely found her footing on the second step. I didn't want to get in trouble when she hurt herself. I said this wasn't such a fun game and told her we should play something else. She said no, it was my turn to jump. I asked if she played Barbies. She didn't answer. I sighed and jumped to the second step.

"There. We're even," I said.

She moved back a few paces to get a running start, then threw herself at the steps. Her feet hit the lip of the third and flew out from under her. Her butt came down hard right before the back of her head hit the concrete with a thwack.

At first she didn't move. It was almost a relief when she started to scream. The adults came rushing out of the house. Nancy's dad scooped her up and pressed her to his chest. Forrestine cooed. Claude folded Nancy's balled-up fists into his big hands. Mom bent to ask me what happened. I explained as quickly as I could. Her grip on my shoulder tightened. She hissed that Nancy was just a little girl. I should have known better. I was ashamed that I hadn't convinced her to quit the dangerous game. I was ashamed of the way her dad held her so tightly in his arms and wouldn't even look at me.

"Those were big changes," Connie says. "Leaving Maine, becoming an older sister, adjusting to a new father."

I nod. "It all happened so fast."

"Do you remember how it felt, being part of a new family in a strange place?"

I used to lie awake at night, eyes wide, pulse racing, afraid of being left behind in the dark. From my twin bed in the room I shared with Sue, I'd track the winding-down sounds of the household. Nancy in the room next door, rocking back and forth in bed long after Mom tucked her in, singing herself to sleep. Dad complaining over the stack of medical charts to be written up. The TV show Sue and Bruce were allowed to stay up and watch. Mom at the back door ordering the dog to hurry up and pee. I wanted desperately to fall asleep while they were still awake. When Sue came to bed she closed the door slowly, slipped silently into her nightgown and slid into the bed next to mine. I knew she was keeping quiet for my sake, but I couldn't resist letting her know that I wasn't asleep. We would whisper for a while, choosing one of our two favorite topics, Christmas or camp. Eventually her end of the conversation trailed off. Then it became imperative to get to sleep before Mom and Dad closed their bedroom door. After that, it was only a matter of minutes before their bathroom tap stopped running, the muffled TV news went silent and darkness suffocated the house.

In their sleep, my family disappeared to a place I couldn't follow. Would they find their way back to me if I called to them? I clamped my eyelids shut and begged to be taken. They were already far ahead. Would I ever catch up?

Every night I'd berate myself for being such a baby, and every night, when I couldn't stand being alone any longer, I'd kick off the covers and feel my way between the beds. Carpet began in the hallway and led to my parents' room. Once I was there, it was hard to find the courage to enter. I stood listening to the sounds of sleep, ashamed of myself for running to Mommy like a toddler. I cracked the door and slipped inside, floating to the far side of the bed where her smell was captured in the jars and bottles on the nightstand. I inhaled the potent clean of her skin and touched her lightly on the arm.

At first she was sympathetic. She hugged me and led me back to bed. She sat with me and rubbed my back. As the nights dragged on and I continued to appear at her bedside, she began to scold. She refused to get out of bed, saying there was nothing more she could do. She sent me back to my room alone, telling me to get my mind off of sleep. "Just think about something else," she snapped. As if I hadn't already tried that and failed a hundred times.

My worries stretched into the daytime. Playing outside in the afternoon, I kept one eye on the sun's position. The dread began to churn in earnest as the shadows of trees lengthened across the yard. I dragged myself inside for dinner, fighting the inevitability of twilight.

Following Dad's prescription, Mom began to add an herbal sleep remedy to the little cup of vitamin supplements I swallowed with juice after meals. She made a point of telling me this, even though she'd never bothered to explain what the other pills were for. She tried to convince me that my troubles were over, that these new pills would make it possible for me to sleep. Nobody asked me why I was afraid.

•

I'M A HALF-DOZEN SESSIONS into therapy when Matteo asks for time apart. I thought I was doing what he wanted by seeing Connie. But it's not enough. He wants me to move out of the house for three months. Because I have no choice, I tell him that I'll do it, but only if we use the time to get reacquainted, with ourselves and one another. He assures me that he still considers us a couple. He describes the arrangement as a courtship. We'll get together three nights a week. We'll go on dates. Sparks will re-ignite. I move across town to a temporary rental. Once I'm out, he tells me he wants to see other women. All I can come up with in protest is that this would be unfair to the other women. They'll think he's single when he's not. I don't say he should be seeing me exclusively. I don't say what I need.

We've been living apart for a little over a month when he goes away for the weekend to visit family in Wisconsin. I ask him if it's OK for me to stay in the house while he's gone. I'm grateful for the chance to sleep in my own bed for a change. On Saturday morning, I decide to tackle the bills that are still in my name. The one from our long distance provider shows dozens of lengthy late-night calls to a number I don't recognize. I check with the company and discover the number belongs to the woman he was seeing when I first met him in Milwaukee. Even so, I can't be sure he's cheating on me.

When I call that afternoon I tell him what I've found and ask if he's broken our agreement. The contempt in his voice is serrated. The old friend he's been talking to is in the middle of family troubles, he explains. He has merely been consoling her. Regardless of the content, I argue, the frequency, length and lateness of the calls suggest a deep intimacy. He's been cultivating that closeness with someone else while holding me at arm's length. He doesn't respond. I let him know I'm moving back into our house. The experiment is over.

I sleep in the guest room downstairs. He rages at me for not keeping my word, for reneging on my pledge to stay away the full three months. He accuses me of inventing any excuse to get out of my depressing rental.

My visits with Connie have emboldened me to stick to my decision. I try to steer clear of his tantrums, but the thought of standing firm through a protracted stalemate makes me queasy. Early one morning, after I hear his alarm clock, I creep in and kneel on the edge of our bed. I tell him I want to fight for our relationship. I tell him it's time to decide whether or not he will join me in this fight. I plead with him to recognize the risk I'm taking, speaking these things aloud, forcing the issue. Somehow I manage to add the condition that if he chooses to stay he will have to commit to couples counseling. I quaver through these things on my knees. My legs wouldn't have held if I'd tried to say them standing up.

He fumes for days. Then he says he'll stay.

We start seeing a couples therapist. We take turns talking to her. Sometimes we actually talk to each other. Our progress is slow and fragile, but it's progress. Connie congratulates me for getting us to this point. She says now it's time to deal with the plane crash, although I still don't see what that has to do with any of this. I don't dispute that the accident affected my adolescent life, my adolescent self. But adolescence and impending middle age are different planets. Or they should be. I should have evolved.

"Until you address that trauma," she insists, "you'll only get so far in any relationship."

I'm startled to hear her use the word trauma. Nothing about my story feels traumatic. It's just oppressive. Harder and harder to carry.

She lets me know that she presented my history to her consulting group. She's excited to share their recommendation. There is a relatively new treatment that one of her colleagues is trained to practice. It has a strange name, abbreviated to a string of initials. She can barely get the letters straight, much less tell me what they stand for. She's pretty fuzzy on how the whole thing works, and can't really give me an idea of what to expect. All she knows is that another of her clients tried it and got excellent results. She thinks it could help me, too.

The therapy Connie wants me to try is called EMDR. I discover online that the letters stand for Eye Movement Desensitization and Reprocessing. I read those words and start to sweat. Desensitization and reprocessing are scary words, especially taken together, like brain and washing. The one thing I prize about myself is my mind. I consider everything below my neck an afterthought, a pedestal for displaying my intellect. No way will I put that in jeopardy.

The first link my search produces takes me to the rant of a man claiming EMDR ruined his life. His therapist wasn't trained to use the protocol, but they decided to give it a whirl anyway. The man believes that a single treatment trapped him in a state of intense agitation from which he's been unable to escape. The scared me worries EMDR really did screw him up. But the part of me that wants this therapy to work notices he's not the most credible guy on the internet.

I click next on EMDR.com and wind up at the official site of the EMDR Institute. Curious to know who does this stuff, I hit the link to find a clinician. It takes me to a database of EM-

DR-certified therapists across the country, searchable by city. I type in some of the remotest places I can think of, certain there will be no desensitization or reprocessing going on in the far reaches of Alabama or North Dakota. But each search turns up multiple practitioners. If this is some kind of scam, a whole lot of people are in on it. I hit the FAQ tab and scroll through a bunch of jargon, patching together a vague sense of the methodology. There are lateral eye movements, and these somehow help the patient "reformulate" negative beliefs.

It still sounds like brainwashing to me, and I'm still terrified of something altering how beautifully I think. I need a medical perspective on EMDR, and I want it quickly, so I go to Dad. I have to know if, physiologically speaking, there's even a remote chance that chunks of my mind will be reprocessed to mush. Dad laughs at my ignorance. My neurons aren't nearly as vulnerable as I suspect, he says. Mom thinks the therapy is an avenue worth exploring and offers to help me pay for my sessions. Matteo shrugs and says, why not? Which translates to, it can't make things any worse.

•

SINCE NO ONE IS raising the kinds of objections I hoped they would, I decide to meet with Connie's colleague, Jan Cehn. I tell myself that a meeting isn't a commitment to treatment. It's simply more research. Jan isn't fazed by the barrage of questions I unload on her. After the smoke clears and it's her turn to talk, I learn that, like Connie, she's a licensed clinical social worker, and that she trained with Francine Shapiro, the psychologist who developed EMDR therapy and founded the institute. Jan says she uses EMDR with about a third of her clients at some point in the course of their work together. It's one of many therapeutic tools she finds helpful.

"Everyone has a different experience with it," she tells me. "It's not a one-size-fits-all approach."

I feel a twinge of disappointment. I've come prepared to do battle with a crusader bent on recruiting me to her cause. But this sensible woman isn't on a soapbox. She scrawls my case history on page after page of a legal pad and allows only that EMDR might be helpful to me. She doesn't promise anything.

She asks if I'd like to see how it works. I'm too curious to refuse. She explains that the eye movement part of the treatment continues to evolve. When she started, she used her index finger to draw her clients' eyes back and forth. Now she uses sound to get the same effect as eye movements. She hands me a small box like a transistor radio with headphones attached. She shows me the volume dial and the controls for speeding up or slowing down the tempo. I put on the headphones. She switches on the machine and asks me to find the settings that feel most comfortable. I listen as an electronic tone pings from one ear to the other—left, right, left, right. I gradually lower the volume and slow the beat and look up to let her know I'm ready.

She turns off the device and tells me to close my eyes. She wants me to visualize a place where I feel secure. Once I have a clear image of this safe place, she says, we'll use the tones to help fix it in my mind. If I ever need a time-out during a session, we'll call up my safe place and I can get some relief there.

I picture the guest room in our house. Matteo and I call it the cave because it's so quiet and dark. We laid soft wool carpeting underfoot and painted the walls a pinkish-brown, the color on the undersides of clouds just after sunset. My body loosens, feeling the pull of the room's containment and comfort.

Then the tones burst in. I startle in my seat and hear myself laugh nervously. My eyeballs begin marching back and forth behind their lids. I imagine what they must look like from Jan's perspective, clanging like a cartoon metronome. A Kit Kat clock drifts into my safe place, round white eyes with black slits for irises flicking back and forth with the pendulum tail. I snort at the silliness of the image and try to settle back into the calm of the cave. After another few seconds, Jan switches off the tones and asks for a report.

"What made you laugh?" she wants to know.

I assume everybody's eyes move during this exercise and tell her about the Kit Kat clock. She assures me that my eyeballs were not moving. We do it again, to reinforce the image of the safe place, and I hold my fingertips against my eyelids to see for myself. She's right. Although the sensation is just as strong, my eyes aren't actually moving.

Jan explains that, should I continue with EMDR therapy, I will likely remember all kinds of things during our sessions. Some of these forgotten experiences may become very present, very real, she says, as if they're happening right now. I tell her about when I was nineteen and had my wisdom teeth pulled in the hospital. I lay on a gurney bobbing toward consciousness while the anesthetic loosened its grip. Without warning, I was in the plane, falling. I kicked wildly, threw my arms out to brace myself and shouted, "No! No! No!" A nurse punched a needle into my butt. Next thing I knew, my parents were standing over me, Dad saying, "Wake up now, time to wake up." My tongue explored the ripped corners of my mouth, crusted with blood. My lips were papery and dry. I felt my face swelling painfully and blinked several times to pull the present into focus. This time is not that time, I told myself. This hospital is not that hospital.

"The body remembers what we've been through," Jan explains. "And those memories can be triggered in a way that drags us back."

It happened again in Paris. I was crossing a subway grate and the smell of raw fuel buckled my knees. I staggered out of the flow of sidewalk traffic and steadied myself against a building. After several deep breaths, I persuaded myself to walk on. I have always walked on. Now, sitting in Jan's office, I realize the time has come to stay put and take a long look. At the accordianned fuselage, the busted bodies, the dead girl. It's time to comb the wreckage.

I book my next session. The blood rushes out of my head when I stand to leave. As I grip the back of my chair to steady myself, Jan hands me a sheaf of Xeroxed pages.

"These might answer more of your questions," she says.

On top of the stack is an interview with Francine Shapiro. I sit down to read it as soon as I get home, still zipped into my jacket. Shapiro describes for her interviewer the walk she was taking in a park one day, preoccupied by distressing thoughts. Suddenly those thoughts left her mind. When she called them back, they weren't nearly as emotionally potent as they'd been moments before. She began to pay closer attention to what was happening as she walked. The next time her mind seized on an upsetting thought, she noticed her eyes begin to move rapidly back and forth on their own. The thought went away. When she brought it back, it too had lost much of its charge.

Shapiro began experimenting, first on herself, then on friends, family and volunteers, testing and revising her eye movement theory and getting similar outcomes. In the protocol she developed, the patient holds a traumatic event in mind while the therapist guides his eyes rapidly back and forth. Shapiro hypothesized that, when the eyes move this way, as in REM sleep, a cross-brain wave pattern is produced that allows a person to both access memories of a trauma and process the emotions surrounding it. Memories that the brain otherwise keeps heavily guarded and out of reach, sometimes even as it replays them over and over, like an endlessly spooling reel of film.

The recurring nightmares that often plague those with PTSD are part of that endless film loop. They are also evidence of the body's attempts to heal itself, Shapiro believes. During REM sleep, the unconscious dredges up the things that are troubling us to be processed and resolved. For a trauma survivor, what surfaces is often so disturbing she wakes before the REM cycle is complete, before healing can occur. By contrast, EMDR therapy activates this self-healing mechanism in a conscious, wakeful patient who can be guided to target specific memories, hold them in mind and complete the cycle.

In other words, EMDR gives a patient waking access to her

brain's projection booth so she can study a disturbing memory frame by frame. Once she's desensitized to it, instead of seeing the memory projected larger than life on a giant screen, she can bring it down to actual size. Rather than occupying more space in her mind or having more immediacy than other memories, the reprocessed memory of the trauma becomes, in effect, just another bad memory. It doesn't disappear, nor is its impact on her life dismissed. It's simply brought down to scale. It's made manageable.

I toss the interview onto the coffee table and slump back against the sofa cushions. It all sounds incredibly reasonable. So why am I still so afraid?

•

I TRIP ON MY way into Jan's office for the second time, dread making me clumsy. I want assurances that what happens in this room will not hurt more than I can stand. How do I steel myself for memories, like body blows, I can't anticipate?

She promises we'll take things one step at a time, together. We sit facing one another, my stomach alive with bees, rising furious in my throat. She untangles the cord and hands me the headphones. She checks her notes for the settings I selected last time, adjusts the dials and asks if the volume and tempo still feel comfortable. I nod. She switches off the machine and tells me to take a few deep breaths. Then she asks me what I remember about the day of the accident. I run through my standard story points. The visit with family in Maine, Dad flying us home, the carbon monoxide putting us to sleep, crashing in someone's back yard. Nancy killed instantly, Mom barely alive, my arm freed by the firemen just before the amputation team arrived.

"Let's back up," Jan says. "How did the day begin?"

I'm used to starting with the flight to Maine. I have to think for a minute about what came before that.

"We left church early," I begin to remember.

"Good. Close your eyes and see if you can put yourself there."

She turns on the machine. I picture our church. White walls, gray linoleum floor, folding chairs. The plain wooden cross behind the podium. Then details start to fill in. Row upon row of the backs of people's heads, the pastor in the pulpit standing over them. My thumb in the hymnal. It's almost time to go.

"Wow," I say when she cuts the tones. "It's almost like I'm there."

"Good," she says. "What do you see?"

The tones click on. Mom and Dad hanging up their robes in the choir room. A blaze-orange windsock at the edge of the tarmac. Tedd in a trench coat waiting for us at the other end. His dining room windows hung with filmy curtains, everyone loading their plates.

"It's weird," I tell Jan. "Vivid. How can things I haven't thought about in forever seem so familiar?"

"It works that way for most people. Just go with what comes up," she advises, refiring the tones.

We slip out during the final hymn, before the benediction, and drive straight to the airfield, still in our church clothes. Mom has sandwiches packed in a cooler for us to eat on the plane. She says this is probably the last time we'll see Aunt Mary, who is moving to the Philippines to become a missionary. She plans to die over there. Mom thinks it's only right to say our final goodbyes in person. Dad wants to keep the visit brief. So do I. I made them promise we'd be back in time for my youth group meeting tonight.

Dad unlocks the cockpit and I crawl in behind him to unlatch the passenger side. Nancy elbows her way in beside me. Mom hands in the cooler first, then climbs up next to Dad.

Dad has been taking us up in small planes for years. It used to be exciting, but not anymore. I still like eavesdropping on the back-and-forth code talk with the control tower, though. Victory Zulu Hotel. Yankee Foxtrot Niner. Hearing the names of the different planes. Beechcraft Bonanza. Piper Comanche. This time we're flying a royal blue Navion Rangemaster, tail number Two Four One Two Tango, on loan, Dad brags, from a direct descendant of Ralph Waldo Emerson. Big deal. I'm not impressed. Half the people in our town claim to be related to Emerson or Thoreau. Besides, we're still on family time here, which is annoying no matter whose plane it is or where we go together. I'd rather be alone in my room or out with my friends. That's why I asked Dad if we could fly instead of drive. It's much faster, and I want to get this visit over with as quickly as possible.

"I didn't want to go to Maine in the first place," I blurt when the tones stop. "I hated family time."

"Good. Go with that," Jan says, punching the machine back on.

I'm wearing the burgundy print skirt I made, cowboy boots, my black sweater. I want to remember what Nancy's wearing, but I can't see it.

On the ground in Portland, Dad makes a display of chocking the tires and knotting the mooring lines just so. Tedd is waiting in front of the terminal, leaning against his car, hands bunched in his coat pockets. We eat a second lunch at his house. The dining room table is set buffet style with an acre of food. There are dark trails matted into blue carpeting. We sit in the living room balancing plates on our laps. Aunt Mary stakes out the piano bench, stick-straight with her back to the keys. The patchwork cardigan draped over her shoulders only partly covers the crepe-paper flesh of her arms. The too-bright colors and loose knit of the sweater make it look like an afghan, so homespun and friendly on my unapproachable aunt, and so ugly, I can't stop staring.

No chair feels comfortable. She is going away to die and no one's talking about it. The whipped potatoes land sad in my stomach and stick. We sing hymns. I try to put Mom in the room but can't see her.

Jan cuts the tones.

"I want the story to go the way I'm used to," I tell her. Without things like sad food and depressing songs. I don't like the way it's filling in.

"That's what happens when we do this," she says. "The way you've thought about stuff changes. Let's keep going."

Weak afternoon light casts no shadow as we drive across town. On the windy tarmac, I pick up a scent of storm. Dad says it's nothing, although back at Tedd's house he used the forecast as an excuse to keep the visit from trailing on. My stomach makes a thrilling lurch toward my crotch as we lift off into sky the color of a bruise. Dusk haloes Mom's profile like blue energy. I picture dipping an arm in up to the shoulder and drawing it back electric.

The red flashes of the port side wing light ricochet off the cloud bank. My eyelids sag. I unclip my lap belt and bend over to nap, batting Nancy's hands away. She pokes my calf. I jab a fist blindly in her direction. Fending her off as I fall asleep.

The pressure in my ears changes. The signal that we're on approach for landing. My brain says, "Seat belt!" But my body won't respond.

Someone nudging my knee. What's your name? he asks. Do you know where you are? How old are you? What's your name? His voice is far away, calling through water. I can't think how to answer. If I could just open my eyes.

She stops the tones. I tell her I'm on the ground, in the dark. She makes a note and urges me on.

The silhouette of a head, bright light behind it.

"What's your name?" The voice is closer, clearer.

"Am I in a car?" I ask, smelling fuel.

"You're in an airplane. There's been an accident."

An accident. What happened?

"My name is Carol," I say.

"Don't worry, Carol. We'll get you out of there."

"I can't move my arm."

Trapped. I can't move my arm!

"What's going on?" Jan asks.

97

The tears come in sheets of salt and snot. I can hardly breathe. I sob, hands balled to fetal fists.

"I can't get out!"

"You're OK," she says. "Stay with it."

My arm is going to explode. Too much pressure bearing down. Then a sudden release. Pins and needles up and down my side.

"My arm's free," I tell her. "Someone grabbed my hand."

They want to put me on a stretcher. I tell the man I'm too heavy. It's going to be all right, he says. The ER doctors lean over me in shrieking light. Dad's in surgery, one tells me. Mom might not make it. Nancy's dead. It's dark on the Children's Ward. Humid and smothering. People stream in to see me. They stand over the bed looking, not touching. I'm so lonely it burns. I can't have Mom. The day nurse washes my hair. I like having her close.

Another wave of tears. The weeping bends me in half. I look up at Jan for a lifeline. She pulls air deep into her lungs, reminding me to breathe. I manage a few shallow sips between sobs. She waits, watching my face. Maybe I'm not supposed to cry this much. When I gather enough breath to speak, I tell her I'm ready to continue. She explains that, for the few minutes we have left, we'll use the tones to create a transition. To clear a space where I can collect myself and prepare to walk out the door.

She slows the tempo. "Keep breathing. Deep inhales and long, slow exhales," she says. "Concentrate on the way your body feels. Try letting go of everything else."

After the intensity of remembering, it's a relief to focus on right now. But every time my chest begins to lift and my throat muscles relax, another spasm shakes loose from my diaphragm, releasing a fresh round of tears.

"It's OK, Carol," she says. "You don't have to hold back anymore."

Her permission makes me cry harder. When the choking and shuddering finally subside, we add words to the breathing and the tones. She wants me to repeat to myself that none of these remembered things can hurt me anymore.

"Keep telling yourself that you're safe now," she says. "You got out of there."

The words flood me with comfort. How can that be? They're just words. But she's right. I did get out. I am safe now. Fresh tears well from the release of saying so. It feels like we've begun to break a powerful spell. My ribs expand. My throat unlaces. I yawn.

"Good work today," Jan says. "We'll do more next week."

Out on the street, as I pull away from the curb, I catch myself humming.

•

MATTEO IS ON A three-month assignment in Italy, where his company is opening a new office. It's crucial to convey the progress I'm making while he's away, to convince him that the sessions with Connie and Jan are working. If I'm even a tiny bit better this week than last, perhaps he'll start loving me again. We schedule phone calls across nine time zones and I deliver improvement reports. I work hard to sound cheerful, slipping in this or that anecdote to illustrate how I've advanced since our last conversation. I tell him something important is shifting inside me. He says he'll believe it when he sees it. I don't fault him for this. It will take a lot of hard evidence to persuade him I can change course, do better, make something of myself. I haven't produced anything concrete yet to justify faith in me. I should have a good job. I should be making a real financial contribution. Until then, I deserve his skepticism.

Still, I wish I could have his companionship as I grope along, tethered to Jan's headset. I want him to know what it's like in there. The terrible press of the dark, the clawing fear. I want him to be amazed at the furious weeping and the words that finally quelled it. I imagine lying beside him in the gray of early morning and recounting my dreams. Jan has asked me to write them down. The night after our first session, I found myself back in the rocking chair at the foot of my parents' bed. They were pronouncing punishment for another bad thing I'd done. But this time it was my adult self in the hot seat. When Mom announced that I'd have to attend Bible study to atone, instead of giving in, I argued that the penalty made no sense. "You want me to believe in the Bible," I told her. "But I don't. Using it as punishment will only make it worse."

I imagine rolling onto my side to tell him what I think this dream means. I'm starting to assert my apartness from my parents, my separateness. Maybe I'm ready to insist they accept me on my own terms. Gently, then, I would rest my hand on his chest and ask, "Do I please you, doing this work, lifting the heavy stones and searching beneath each one?"

•

JAN UNWINDS THE CORD, hands me the headset, checks the settings and asks if I'm ready to begin. We've booked a longer appointment this week. From now on, sessions will last ninety minutes instead of sixty. "That'll give us more time to really delve into things," she explains. But I suspect it's because she's worried about me crying so much I won't be able to stop myself at the end of an hour.

She sends me back to the day of the crash, directing me to start early in the day and move forward from there. She switches on the tones.

Dad stands at his bureau, loading his pockets. Pens, utility knife, comb, handkerchief. I'm sweetly asking him if we can fly instead of driving. Tedd's living room in the dark Portland house, shaded around the edges. Nancy skittering into the hallway in stocking feet with my niece, Jacki, close at her heels. I'm marooned on the couch, surrounded by dumb talk. I can't wait to leave. The airplane on the tarmac, blue with yellow tail numbers. Once we're airborne, the afternoon overcast fades to blue dusk beyond the windows. Mom turns to glare over her left shoulder at me, telegraphing the message, Behave! I yank my trench coat over my head, unbuckle the seatbelt and double over to sleep. Radio patter crackles in the background, fuzzy and indistinct. I can hear Dad bellow, "We're going in!" as we torpedo through the trees. But that can't be right.

"What's happening?" Jan asks.

"I remembered Dad saying something like 'We're going

to crash.' But he couldn't have. He would have been unconscious."

"Good," says Jan. "You're sorting it out. Keep going."

I can't wake up. My brain paws through sludge. There's a heavy tang of fuel in my nostrils, metallic on my tongue. Dad's voice at my feet. Then silence, saturated black. Then the man with the bright hair is asking questions in a thick Boston accent. He wants to know my name. He wants me to tell him what day it is.

"Where is your ahhm?" he asks.

I sense its numb throbbing, but I can't reach it with my free hand. It's twisted behind me, and pinned. I should be able to direct him to it. I should be responding faster. He's frustrated with me. I should at least be giving better answers. He's trying so hard.

"Which arm was trapped?" Jan asks, cutting the tones. "Right or left?"

"Left," I tell her. "Wait. No, my right."

"Your writing arm," she says, and makes a note, finding some significance in that. But I don't pick up the thread. I'm stuck on something else. I'm worried about how different it feels this time. When she first brought me back here, the terror of waking in the smashed cockpit gutted me. I couldn't stop sobbing. But revisiting the same scene today, I'm sifting through the rubble dry eyed. I decide this means I'm doing something wrong. I tell Jan I must be holding back somehow.

"Those intense feelings, or different ones, might crop up again later on," she tells me. "Or they may simply be gone."

Her delivery is matter-of-fact. But I'm not ready for the

panic to be gone. Something in me needs this process to be protracted and punishing. It's too soon to feel . . . what? Less heavy. Less weighed down by all there is to carry, like I'm shedding a wardrobe of lead-lined clothing one glove, one sock, one coat sleeve at a time. I haven't earned this relief.

Jan says, "You're doing great. Let's keep going."

The noise of rescue comes in bursts. Men shouting, running, a generator firing. The crushing weight on my arm springs away. I'm yanked into the light, lifted high on a stretcher. The crowd gasps. Tubes and IV bags swing above me in the ambulance. The blur of familiar faces in the ER waiting area as they wheel me through. Our pastor follows the doctors into the exam room. The catalog of casualties skates over me. The pastor leans close, his eyes doling out sadness. When he mouths how sorry he is, how very sorry, his grief pelts my chest like pebbles. The blanket at the foot of the gurney is too far to reach.

A rolling series of fluorescent lights. Flat on my back in an elevator. Colored footprints on the ceiling. A hard stop in a warm hallway. Voices I don't recognize wonder what they're supposed to do with me. Another voice announces that there is nowhere else to put me, so they'll have to make do.

"What makes you think they didn't want you on the Children's Ward?" Jan asks.

"It was obvious." They stashed me in an empty room, heaved me into a cold bed and left me there.

"Was it because you weren't hurt badly enough?"

"Not by a long shot!" Just a swollen head and some cuts and bruises. No busted ribs, no punctured lung, no internal hemorrhage. Not a single broken bone. And I was the one who wasn't belted in.

They won't let me go to the bathroom. Of the four beds, mine is closest to the corridor and the toilet I'm forbidden to use. Again and again, a needle of light stabs one eye, then the other. The night nurse retreats without so much as a hand pat. Morning thrums in my temples. Faith is there, beside the bed. Tidying the nightstand, smoothing and re-tucking the sheets. "We have crayons if you want to color today," she teases. When she comes to tell me I'm being released, I think she's still kidding around. She gets me ready to visit Mom and Dad.

"What's making you cry now?" Jan asks.

I'm looking for my mother beneath the bandages and the tubing, tears running down my neck as the tones keep their steady beat. I see the waxy pad of her cheek, one eye, the sharp point of her nose, a curl of lip visible through gauze. What if she doesn't recognize me, after everything that's happened?

"Did you cry then, at your mother's beside?"

No, I guess not.

And now I'm out. Padding through Vi's nighttime house. Waiting at the end of the long drive for a school bus with an unfamiliar route. Dad in a barber cape in Vi's basement. I want to leave him there, let him find his own way back upstairs to the kitchen. But I brush away the snipped hairs and help him out of the chair. We take Mom home to our own house, where I can't stop picturing our bathtub filled with blood.

"I wish I had some comfort there, some company," I tell Jan.

"You're not alone here," she reminds me.

I nod and swipe at a fresh batch of tears.

"You haven't told me how Nancy died," she says.

The impact of the crash yanked the seatbelt through her middle like the flat of a blade. It severed a main artery. She bled to death. A carpet of Astroturf around her open grave like a poncho. Dad's arm hangs heavy in the crook of a sling. Mom can't stand by herself, so Sue and I take turns propping her up. Grammy's eyes are flat, like she's been slapped. Her posture is crumpled, but her face in the rain looks young. As I listen to the tones, Grammy's face becomes my youth group leader's face, slick with tears on the night of the crash, when he drew up a chair beside the bed. The uncurtained look in his eyes confirms Nancy is gone. He sits close, holding my hand. His watching me, cradling me in his gaze, makes me want to cry, but without the crushing feeling at the base of my windpipe. The room isn't as dark around us as it was the last time I looked.

"Something just went away in my chest," I tell Jan. "Just now, something let go." A chunk of iceberg hissing into the sea.

"How does it feel?" she asks.

"Peaceful."

•

I'M ABOUT TO TURN forty. Matteo invites me to join him in Europe to celebrate my birthday. Ten days before leaving, I dig out the poetry collection I've been revising off and on since graduate school. A friend has introduced me to the editor of a small press who's agreed to look at my manuscript. I rush to polish it one more time, reordering sections and splicing in a few newish poems before dropping it in the mail. I know nothing will come of it. I'm simply being paid a professional courtesy. Still, it's important to be able to report that I've done something.

I fly to Milan. We spend the weekend with his family. I struggle to follow the flow of conversation. He translates as we stagger from one lavishly spread table to the next. Cousins, neighbors, bar buddies, old ladies smelling of camellia all tell me how different I look since the last time we visited. Younger, they say, and happier. Part of this is prettification, the national pastime of Italy. But it's also possible that they're responding to what I've noticed lately in myself: a steady relinquishing of layers, an unfamiliar buoyancy.

He translates their compliments without comment. At night, after dinner, he watches the soccer match on TV or goes out with the other men to close the bars. It irks me that the women aren't invited. I want to incite a revolt. We could sit up late ourselves in the kitchen, emptying bottles of fizzy wine from the cellar. Instead I shower and climb into bed with a book.

After Milan we fly to Paris, where he has arranged to do business for the week. We stay in a fourth floor walk-up in the Marais. He rides the Metro to the office in the mornings. I head out to collect produce and cheeses from the market stalls, or to track down the perfect croissant, its wrapping translucent with butter by the time I set it on a café counter beside my espresso.

With days mostly to myself, I retrace familiar routes through gardens and arcades, down puddled cobblestone lanes and along the broad wet sidewalks lining the boulevards. A poem from my manuscript follows me as I cross and re-cross the Seine. It began as an assignment to inhabit the persona of a literary character. I chose Icarus, re-imagining him as a daughter intent on pleasing her father, eager to earn her wings. I can't shift the poem out of my head. I decide I'm going to show it to Connie and Jan when I get back to California.

After spending each day alone, I look forward to meeting my man for drinks and dinner. Strolling home tipsy together through Parisian streets feels romantic. There may be no passionate lingering in bed, no skin exploring skin in the dark, but I'm grateful he has brought me here.

On our final day together he promises to leave work early so we can have some extra time to celebrate my birthday. I cut my wanderings short to be there when he arrives. I've been sitting around for an hour when he phones to say he's running behind and still has one more call to make. My face is burning when I hang up. I push open the windows and glare down the narrow street, hating its tea salon chatter and sauntering couples. Tears leap out, clearing the filigreed railing like suicides. I want to be angry at him. I want to be blind, spitting furious, and I think for a moment that I might be. But I don't really know how. Frustration and hurt are easy. Why is anger so hard? He does this, calling at the last minute to change the plan. His job is more important to him than I am. When it's me or his work, I never win.

Nothing has changed. I resign myself to an afternoon of brooding and sighs. But something weird starts happening in my head, like pinballs pinging through my brain. My thoughts are jumping their tracks, steaming down a new line. I can't believe how sick I am of holding my tongue. Every time I get pissed off I tell myself it's not worth making a fuss. I never blow my stack. I don't say what I want. I don't have a clue how to ask for what I need. I act like I don't deserve a blessed thing. I'm just a six-foot bag of skin taking up space, breathing borrowed air.

I wipe my nose, pull on a sweater and carom down four flights of stairs to the street. The sun has come out enough to suggest a sunset. I head toward the river, crossing to the île de Saint-Louis. I lap the periphery of the island first, then plunge down the middle, past antique shops and cheese mongers and the perpetual queue for ice cream at Bertillon. The day's last light reflects off the Seine, brightening the evening rush. The backside of Notre Dame comes into view, its most honest angle, with the architecture exposed. I draw the scene into my lungs in deep draughts, waiting until no trace of crimson remains beyond the domes and steeples punctuating the sky.

When I return to the apartment he is there, ready with the standard defense. He couldn't help it, there was work to be done. We're so accustomed to this routine, he expects to coast through my accusing silence to the usual "How was your day?" exchange, our shorthand for, Let's just forget about it. But there will be no coasting today.

"That excuse just isn't good enough," I hear myself say, resisting the urge to back away and watch what happens from a safer distance. "We made plans to do something special. When you commit to something like that, I expect you to keep your word."

A fountain of cortisol lets loose in my gut. But I keep going. I tell him what I've been learning in therapy about the ways I elect to suffer, about how I punish myself. I tell him I'm determined to stop doing these things. I say out loud that I am not expendable. That I am a top priority and deserve to be treated like one. I tell him he needs to manage his job commitments better in cases like this, when I should take precedence over his work.

A full-body flush of elation seizes me once these words are out and cannot be retracted. I have not come remotely close to saying, Goddammit! This is my birthday celebration and you're supposed to act like you love me! Still, it feels like a stay of execution to have said anything at all.

I fly home excited to resume my sessions with Connie and Jan. When a dozen roses get delivered to the house, I'm embarrassed at first by his extravagance. I tell myself it's too much. I don't deserve such a grand gesture. Then something inside me bristles. Oh please, cut the shit! What are you, a starving mutt who winces every time somebody chucks her a bone? My answer is so quiet I can only hear it with my heart.

Yes.

•

THE POEM I BRING to therapy is in three parts, one for each of the three times in childhood I thought I was going to die. The first time was in a rowboat. The second, in a car. The third, in the airplane. The poem starts, "My father wanted me to fly (or was it to die?) before I was born."

My first father, Arthur Fish, didn't want any more kids when he married my mother. Two sons from his first marriage were enough. But Mom was twenty-six and longed for children of her own. She had three babies by Caesarian section. After Wayne died, the obstetrician told her it would be dangerous to have any more. When she announced that she was pregnant a fourth time, with me, the doctor insisted she stay in bed until her due date. She agreed. She took daily doses of DES. She prayed without ceasing. She talked to her belly and begged the growing bump to keep growing. Arthur Fish pictured a different outcome. His wife was laid up, unable to take care of the two toddlers underfoot. He would have hoped for a miscarriage.

"But that's not what I really want to talk about today," I tell Jan. "I can't get the second part of the poem out of my head."

It's about Dad, father number two. He and I got into a car accident when I was ten. It was the weekend before Mom's birthday. Dad asked me to go with him to the mall, just the two of us. He wanted me to help pick out her birthday present. I didn't feel like going, but I could tell he was making an effort to include me. Maybe because Mom asked him to. "I play along," the poem reads. "I'm ten and yearn to be good." We stopped at a traffic light, then began a left turn into the mall parking lot. A green tank of a station wagon came barreling through the intersection and T-boned us on the passenger side, my side. "Flung hard to the floor, tasting door metal and teeth and raking air for breath, I've already begun to blame myself," the poem admits, "for not warning him in time."

"Why would I think that?" I ask Jan. "Like it's all my fault. He was the one driving. He should have looked."

"Good question," Jan says.

"It seems like I'm taking too much of the blame for stuff like this."

"I'm glad you brought the poem. You've been putting these pieces together for a while. Can we back up to the first part, though, to the boat? Tell me more about that. How old were you?"

I was five. Mom, Bruce, Sue and I spent that summer in a converted boathouse on Castine Harbor. It was built on stilts, so the tide would come in beneath us. There was a doll-sized kitchen downstairs. We all slept in one big bedroom upstairs facing the water. My cot was set up under a bank of windows. Before falling asleep, I'd lie on my back pretend-counting stars. In the morning, I'd sit on the steps leading down to the beach sipping hot chocolate with my imaginary friends, Connie and Chippy.

"What about your father? Where was Fish?"

He was there sometimes when I woke up on a Saturday. He would stand at the kitchen sink looking out to sea, filling up the room. He built the rowboat to surprise us, scrounging discarded pieces of plywood from the garage at home. He heaved and tugged it to the water's edge, secured the oars, waded in up to his knees, kicked a leg over the side and jumped in. His foot punched a hole straight through the bottom of the boat. Water sluiced in, but he insisted it was still sea worthy. He wanted us kids to use it. When he wasn't around, only Sue and Bruce were allowed. Bruce rowed. Sue sat in front. I had to watch from shore. The oars were heavy and the hull clumsy, so mostly they turned in circles. Mom and I were in the house the day they scraped a barnacled heap of rocks and started hollering. It took all four of us pushing and pulling to get the boat up on dry sand.

Jan unwinds the cord and hands me the headphones. "Good start. Let's take it from there."

Dazzling sunshine at the water's edge. Piles of shells and pebbles deposited by the tide. A dark trail gouged through sand where he's dragged the boat back to the water. I don't hear him coming, but suddenly he's wedging a life vest over my head. I'm lifted from the beach to the rough seat at the stern. He pulls Sue in by the scruff of her neck, straddles the gunwale and shoves off with a sneakered foot. Cold, cold water bubbles in fast. It covers my feet and keeps rising. Salt stinging my shins. A hole so big my head might slip through. I don't know how to swim.

He faces us and strokes. Past where the deep water begins, faster and further from shore. He's been dead for so long, I'd forgotten what he looked like. But the tones pull his face into shrill focus, every muscular twitch. He's laughing.

"You want to go out further, don't you," he says.

We make for the red bell buoy. The sad clang I listen to in bed, lying beneath a quilt that smells like bread.

"This is how you row a boat," he harangues. "Pick a point on shore and stay in line with it." The water comes and comes.

"What was your sister doing?" Jan wants to know.

"I can't see her. I'm too scared to turn and look."

"How about your mother? Where was she?"

"She must be there," I say. I scan the beach for her, my fixed point, but I don't see her.

"So, this was another time you felt alone," Jan offers.

Tears, instant and fierce. He is laughing, mocking me for being afraid. Telling me we are safe when death has me by the feet. My adult hands reach up to claw at the scarf knotted around my neck. Jan asks what's wrong.

"My throat feels so tight," I tell her, pulling at the fabric. "I can't say or do anything. I'm frozen."

As we close on the red buoy, the sound slams my ears. I want to clamp my hands over them, but I'm too terrified to move. He rows around it, leaning hard against the current. Its footing is green with algae, combed and flowing like hair. We turn back toward shore.

"Tell me what you're feeling," Jan says as she cuts the tones.

"Numb. Frightened. Confused. Why is this happening? What did I do wrong?"

"Doesn't sound like you did anything wrong. You weren't even in the boat when it hit the rocks, right?"

"Right."

"But you think you did something wrong."

His face, laughing, furious.

"Let's keep going," Jan says, switching the tones back on.

I want Mom on that beach. I want her pacing back and forth, wading in fully clothed as we approach, grabbing Sue and me, clutching us to her even before the prow of the boat stutters ashore. Instead, I see her gripping a coffee cup in the morning kitchen, her back to the window. I see her miles away, floating motionless, unhearing, in the shallows of our favorite salt pond.

Now she's holding my hand at Sand Beach, propelling me toward the cold surf. Arthur Fish holds my other hand and together they swing me out over the waves, my feet scooping up spray. They make a wheeeeee! sound like this swinging is fun, but it's scary. Then time collapses and the picture shifts. I'm in Mom's hospital room after the plane crash. With one glazed eye fixed on my face, she whispers that this is God's will.

My head gets crowded with all that rushes in to be said. I was so scared! I couldn't find you. I thought I'd never be anything again except alone. Mommy! Where were you? Instead, I sit quietly beside the bed, my hand threading through plastic tubes to grasp her fingers.

"I can't say what I need to. She's barely alive. It wouldn't be fair."

"So, because she was hurt you kept it to yourself."

"She had enough to deal with already."

Mom lying in a dark room on one of her migraine days. Her voice a whisper sending me away.

"Picture yourself with her," Jan says. "What happens when you try saying what's on your mind?"

I pinch my eyes closed. Her hand white against the white sheet. Her one eye roams, finds my face. She's ready for me to say something. But nothing comes.

"I can't. She doesn't deserve it." Part of her is iron. But she's fragile, too. I have to protect that part, not attack it. I'm crying and holding an image of a face streaked with heavy lines. Bars. A wrench tightens around my windpipe.

"I'm choking!" I croak.

Jan nods. "Maybe that's from all the things you don't let yourself say."

•

"WHAT ELSE DO YOU remember about your father?" she asks at the start of our next session.

"Only a handful of moments," I tell her. "They all have the same texture."

I remember crawling into the big bed, burrowing beneath the covers on Mom's side. Drunk on the soapy smell that clung to her from the bath. If I lay completely still he might not notice me. I could stay right there all night, pulling her into my nose as I slept. But he never let me get away with it. He'd throw off the blankets, shovel me out and haul me back to the room I shared with Sue. He'd drop me on my bed and leave me. No tucking in. No kiss goodnight. One time, before dredging me from their bed, he flipped the covers off my head and told me to look at the TV. "This is how we got you out of your mother's stomach," he said. I watched a Q-Tip paint a wet stripe across a jiggly surface. Then a skinny knife traced the path the swab had made. Something like creamy Jello jumped away from the blade, oozing a dark liquid.

"Yikes," Jan says.

"Yeah. He pretty much scared the crap out of me. He used

to steal my food, too."

Every day at lunchtime he would climb the stairs from his medical office, waltz into the kitchen and help himself to half of my sandwich. Every day I begged my mother not to cut it. She ignored me. The moment I heard him on the stairs, I would drape myself over my plate. He'd stand over me laughing, then pry me upright and snap my lunch down his gullet. One day Mom finally gave in to my begging and left the sandwich whole. When he breezed into the kitchen, I was holding it up to my face, bite marks in all four corners. He stopped short and chuckled. He didn't approach until I'd balled up what was left of the sticky middle and plopped it down on my plate.

"Finished?" he asked.

I nodded.

"You've made a real mess," he said, lifting me out of my chair.

On our way to the bathroom we paused in front of the gilt-framed dining room mirror. He insisted I look at myself. Jelly spread from the corners of my mouth to the pads of my cheeks in a demented smile.

"Look at your mess. What a bad girl," he scolded. "Keep those grubby paws off me."

"What a bad girl," he repeated, wiping my face and fingers and rinsing the washcloth in the bathroom sink.

Before a long car trip, he called the three of us kids into the big bedroom and told us to stand at the foot of the bed. He pulled our pants and underpants down around our ankles, pressed us, stomach down, onto the bedspread and gave us each an injection in the butt. A sedative. He needed peace and quiet in the car while he drove.

Sometimes he bounced me on his canoe of a foot while he sat beside his desk, one leg crossed over the other. The rough shoelaces chafed my inner thighs. When he flexed his foot at the bottom of the bounce, my crotch slammed hard against his ankle.

"That's pretty much what I remember about him," I tell Jan. "When he made an appearance, he was big and scary. But most of the time he wasn't there."

"How did he die?"

"Heart attack. He was fifty-nine. I was six."

It was a cold spring afternoon. Sue and I were outside ignoring the babysitter, who had come over that morning when Mom rushed to the hospital without saying why. Sue was straddling the crook of an apple tree in our neighbor's orchard when the big dinner bell that meant "Come home!" began to ring. I was on the ground below, looking up. Sue wouldn't let me climb trees because all I ever did was fall out of them. The ringing got frantic. "Look out!" she said, and I backed away from the trunk to give her room to jump down.

We were standing in the front doorway when Mom came up the walk flanked by Tedd and Allon. It looked like she'd forgotten how to make one foot follow the other. They steadied her up the steps and steered her into the living room. She sank into one of the cane-backed chairs, the ones with crushed velvet cushions. I loved brushing my palm over the fabric, the nap shifting from rough to smooth. Mom was crying hard, a handkerchief with crocheted edges balled in her fist. When she pulled a hanky out of her purse in church, it always smelled of lifesavers and new shoes. She had a lot of purses, each with its own embellished hankie inside. I liked to slip into the hall closet and pull the pocketbooks down from the shelf, open the latches and sink my nose deep into the smell.

Mom dabbed her eyes and gathered us close. Our father was gone to heaven, she said. Gone to be with baby Wayne and Jesus. I ducked my head and stepped through this news like a curtain of water. It registered, then quickly evaporated. We wouldn't see him at all anymore, which wouldn't be that different. What made me cry was my mother's crying. Slumped in the big chair, she was a baby doll with no stuffing in the neck.

The pews were packed for his funeral. The grass at the cemetery was brown. The reception at our cousins' house afterward was so crowded I couldn't find a place to stand. I settled on the stairs, six steps up from the bottom. I watched the adults in the living room, heads thrown back, eyes shut tight in spasms of laughter, paper plates overloaded.

There was a man standing by himself, propped against the wall just inside the front door. He straightened and moved toward me, rested one hand on the banister and one foot on the bottom step.

"It's kind of confusing, isn't it," he said, tracking my gaze around the room. "Some of us like to stand back a while and take it in." We watched the room in silence. Eventually he shifted away and the crowd eddied in around him.

I tell Jan, "That was my introduction to the man who would become my next father."

I don't know where Bruce was, probably in the kitchen eyeing the casseroles. Sue was playing Hot Wheels with our boy cousins in their room. She was secretly relieved. On the day we learned our father was dead, I imagine she drifted out of the living room and paced the empty front hall, tracing a figure eight, letting word spread through her limbs. Arthur Fish was dead. He had been coming to her in the dark as long as she could remember. And now it was over.

Jan's pen skids to a halt on her yellow pad. She's looking up at me like we're meeting for the first time.

"Your older sister? She was sexually abused by your father?" she asks.

"Yes. It's possible he did it to my brothers, too."

Sue was only three when it started. She didn't breathe a word until we were adults and she'd been seeing a therapist for a while. She didn't have clear memories, just a strong feeling. She asked Mom if she could help her understand this feeling, if she could verify what had happened. Mom remembered something, but not about our father. She was looking out the window one afternoon and saw Bruce alone in the yard, without his sister. Standing on the lawn calling Sue's name, she noticed the neighbor's cellar door was open. At the top of the cellar stairs she called again. Sue emerged from the dark with the much older neighbor boy. Arthur Fish brokered an agreement with the boy's parents. No charges would be filed if they sought counseling immediately. Sue was taken to a child psychologist. She told the nice man that the boy had shown her some pictures. The nice man deemed her unscathed by whatever had happened in the cellar.

"So your mom doesn't think anything happened with your father?"

"She doesn't deny it, but she can't really confirm it either. The numbers definitely add up, though. Mom was on bed rest the whole time she was pregnant with me. That had to have been when he started in on Sue."

Jan is fumbling to untangle the headset cord. "OK. Let's see what you remember." She switches on the tones.

I'm in bed, my childhood bed in Maine, on the right side of the room. Sue's bed is on the left. There's a window between our headboards, and a low wooden chest with a lamp. The detail is eerie. *The Big Book of Fairies* on the shelf, the painted porcelain lamb pulling a cart, the wall paper pattern clashing with the bedspreads. Then it's nighttime. I'm lying awake, thinking Sue's asleep. Or maybe she's pretending. I get the feeling she's good at pretending to be asleep. It's so dark I can't see a thing. I hear voices, though. Whispering. He's there, on Sue's side of the room. He shushes her. She whimpers.

"There's a fight going on inside of me," I tell Jan.

She cuts the tones. "What's happening?"

"Part of me feels like what I'm seeing and hearing is true. Part of me thinks I'm just making it up."

"It doesn't matter right this minute," she tells me. "Just keep going."

I breathe deeply and try to settle into the rhythm of the tones. Nighttime. Whispering. The broad curve of his back. He is perched on the edge of the bed opposite, turned away.

Why won't he pay attention to me? The question breaks the surface before I can censor it. Acid backs up in my throat. I rake the headset off my ears, letting it fall into my lap.

"What?" Jan asks.

"It's repulsive. I'm repulsive. I have to stop."

I drop my face into my palms, grinding the heels of my hands into my eyes. She lets me sit for a long moment, then prods.

"Tell me," she says, gently.

"It must be real," I say. "We must be tapping into real feelings. From a time when I was too small to know better."

"About what?"

"What he was doing in there! Had I known what he was doing, I could never, never, never have felt what just came up."

"What did you feel?"

"Envy. Jealousy. Why wouldn't he come to me? He never came to my side of the room. It freaks me out to think that I actually felt that way!"

"Sure," Jan says. "Of course it does, looking back at it now. But like you said, when you were four or five or six years old, you didn't know why your father was in your room at night. You just knew he was there, focused on your sister instead of you. Why wouldn't you want him to pay attention to you? It's what children expect from their parents."

I know she's right. But at this moment, the whole thing just feels filthy. I clutch my arms and long for a scalding shower. Jan asks if I'm OK to continue. I don't want to. The sick churns in my belly when I think about returning to that room. But it feels like I've left unfinished business there. So I close my eyes, let out a long breath and reposition the headphones over my ears.

The tones summon nothing but darkness at first. No hushed voices. No hunched outlines in the dark. I direct my child self to roll onto her side and peer through it, toward Sue's bed. She's noiseless, motionless in the black, but I'm certain she's there. And then it comes in a flood, roiling out of her like toxic smoke, like billowing soot. An immense, yawning sorrow. It smothers me, ash in my nostrils, thick on my tongue. And it keeps coming, curling in the corners of the room, climbing the walls, butting silently against the ceiling. The softest sadness in the world. It's always there. It's what flushed me out of bed so many nights. I'd wake up in the dark at the top of the stairs, or curled against Bruce's warm back. I couldn't sit with it. I left her alone and exposed.

"I didn't protect her," I sob to Jan.

"No, you didn't," she says. "But what could you have done?"

•

A GREEN STATION WAGON is gunning for us, closing in fast. Dad's face stutters sideways, skidding across the frame, then hangs above me. I can't see his eyes, just the dark tint of aviator sunglasses. He's asking if I'm OK. I can't produce enough breath to say yes. I'm on the floor, goose-honking for air. He knows where to hit me to get me breathing again. A hard thwap on the back, just one, between my ribs. I sputter and guzzle oxygen in drunken swigs, then scoot backwards off the floor to what's left of the passenger seat.

He turns the key. The engine wheezes. He steers us out of the intersection. Our whole right side is bashed in. The shark-mouthed Pontiac looks untouched. The driver, a tiny grey-haired lady, stands beside it, too close to passing traffic. A policeman wades into the intersection, glass crunching underfoot. His Polaroid camera spits out evidence. A witness is interviewed. Our car limps home, air rushing in where it shouldn't. I watch the road blur by through a gap in the mangled doorframe.

"Sounds serious. You weren't hurt at all?" Jan asks.

"I should have been."

"How come?"

"Dad loved that car," I tell her. Even at ten I could see how proud he was to own a Mercedes. Buttons for everything. Smooth tan seats that smelled like fancy gloves. Totaled.

"I should have screamed or something, to warn him."

"Why didn't you?"

I was the girl who held back, the one who secretly believed she didn't need a father. He was reaching out, trying to bond with me. He asked me to help him pick out Mom's birthday present, figuring I would warm to him. I went along for Mom's sake, trying to be the family she wanted. But I didn't like being there. With that kind of daughter on board, bad things were bound to happen.

"I was being selfish."

"And you think being selfish made bad things happen," Jan says. "Go with that." She flicks on the tones.

When Mom tells us she is pregnant, she's smiling but seems afraid. Or maybe fear is what I see because I don't want another brother or sister. She makes a point of telling me what a wonderful example I'll be. She's counting on me to help her take care of the baby. I am fourteen, nearing the end of eighth grade. I picture my high school years hijacked by a needy thing. A life of bottling, diapering, potty training. No time for fun.

I am so miserable I finally take a friend's advice and visit the school guidance counselor. To get in to see her, I have to walk through the principal's office, where he sits scowling at me from behind his desk. What the counselor tells me, once she closes the door and sits down next to me, is that pretty much any kid my age would feel the way I do. Making room for a new baby is a difficult adjustment. I welcome her sympathy, but it doesn't change the facts. I've already been knocked out of youngest child position by Nancy. A new baby will seal my fate as the responsible older sister, when what I really want is to be the baby again myself.

Dad is beside himself with excitement. He swaggers with pride. Then one Saturday morning in early summer, we kids wake up to find him sitting alone at the kitchen table. He is unshaven and looks like he dressed in a big hurry. His eyes are glassy and his voice flat as he explains that Mom is in the hospital. She miscarried in the middle of the night. He'd worked on her for hours, trying to calm the contractions, the bed soaking in blood. But nothing helped. She expelled the fetus into the toilet. Then she fainted. He wrapped her in towels and carried her to the car without waking us. She will probably stay in the hospital overnight. She's lost so much blood they want to keep an eye on her for a while. After he tells us these things, he goes upstairs to shower.

We head outside without breakfast. The neighborhood kids are gathering. We sit on the damp grass in the sun and tell them the news. Nobody speaks for a long time. Eventually someone suggests that we might feel better if we ride our bikes for a while. So we do. Huffing up the street to the dead end. Coasting back down the two hills. Around our circular drive-way and up to the dead end again. A family friend comes to strip the bloody sheets and clean up the mess in the bathroom. She makes us lunch and brings it outside. We sit at the pic-nic table eating sandwiches that are thinner than Mom's and drinking juice out of paper cups.

In the late afternoon, I make sure not to let the screen door slam behind me as I slip inside to pee. Dad is sitting at the kitchen table with Al Frizzell. He is crying, and although he tries to cover it up when I come in, he can't stop. What strikes me most, however, is the vase of fresh-cut tiger lilies in the middle of the table. They're from next door, delivered by a neighbor after word of what happened travelled down the street. As far as I know, she's never cut her prized flowers be-fore. I slip wide-eyed past the flaming bouquet, orange tongues curled back from darkly speckled mouths. Dad's voice fills the space, murky with tears. When I reach the cool hallway be-yond the kitchen, I pause and smile. Mom has lost buckets of blood and Dad is weeping in the kitchen, but I stand smiling in the dim passage. There will be no baby.

"What kind of sick reaction was that?" I ask Jan. "With Mom in the hospital and Dad sobbing in the kitchen, all I could think about was my disgusting self."

"That doesn't make what happened your fault."

"Maybe not, but it sure makes me a bad daughter."

I'm lying on my bed reading. It's a weekend afternoon. The house is loud around me, but I'm tucked into a quiet corner. Mom pokes her head in the door. I hold my book in front of my face. "Knock, knock," she says. I peek up from the page and she takes the opening. She could sit on Sue's bed and be close enough, but she settles on mine. The mattress sags so my hip rolls into hers. I pull away.

She wants to talk about my participating more in family activities. Her face is flushed. She's been jabbing the vacuum cleaner across the downstairs carpet, working up the nerve to say this. She reminds me that I used to like it when we did things together. Now I'm mopey and withdrawn. "Where'd my happy girl go?" she wants to know. Her eyebrows are raised halfway between hurt and hope. I want to say the right thing. I can't tell her I think family time is a drudge. When I do stuff, I want to do it with my friends. I wish she would just give my hand a squeeze and let this go.

"Mom's mad at me. I'm a disappointment," I tell Jan. I haven't learned to love Dad like a good daughter, to love Nancy like a good sister. Sue, on the other hand, joins in without eye rolling or heavy sighs. I keep willing myself to be more like her, but it doesn't take.

The first time I found a smudge of blood in my underwear, I burst into the kitchen with the news. Mom was pulling a casserole out of the oven. "You know where the pads are," she said, sounding annoyed. "You're supposed to be helping me get supper on the table."

"Hold onto that feeling that you're a disappointment," Jan tells me. "Take it back to the plane crash and see what comes up."

I'm cramped. I want to stretch my legs but can't without kneeing the back of Dad's seat. I want to be home, finished with this stupid trip. I want Nancy to keep her damn hands to herself. I'm cold. I pull my trench coat tighter around me, clutching the lapels in a fist against my chest. I lean forward, pressing my face between the front seats. Half-shouting to be heard, I ask for more heat.

My eyes burst open. "Bingo!"

"What?" Jan asks, cutting the tones. "What happened?"

"Dad turned on the heat because I asked him to!"

"And? Why bingo?"

"That's how the gas got into the cabin! The carbon monoxide. Dad says it came through the heater. When I asked for heat, I brought it in."

"I see."

"I'm the one who did it! I caused the crash. And Dad said I saved his life. What a joke!"

"OK, hold on," Jan says, settling back into her chair. "If you hadn't felt cold during that flight, someone else would have. Sooner or later someone would have asked for some heat."

I cross my arms. She presses me. "What are you feeling right now?"

"Like it was all my fault."

"That's a guilty thought. Obviously. Where do you feel that guilt in your body?"

"My stomach. And my chest. My ribs are squeezing shut."

"How strong is the feeling on a scale of one to ten?"

"Strong. At least a ten."

"How about the car accident. Is the feeling in your chest and stomach there, too?"

"In the car, yes. In the boat, too."

"Good. Great." She reaches for the controls. "I want you to try something. Try considering that you're not completely at fault for all these things. Hold on to that possibility while you listen to the tones."

Dad's standing at his bureau, scooping coins into his pocket. It won't take much to get my way. If we have to go, I say, can we at least fly?

"I manipulated Dad to get what I wanted," I tell Jan. "I was being selfish."

"Like any kid."

"That's no excuse. Nancy died!"

"I don't see what you did wrong that needs excusing. It was normal to want to be with your friends."

I shake my head no.

"Why is it so hard to think this way, that it's not all your fault? What happens when you try to allow it?"

I picture Dad combing his hair in the mirror. He doesn't want to go, either. He thinks our Maine relatives are hicks. He thinks this trip is a waste of a good Sunday. So do I. But Mom wants us to go as a family.

"My throat is so tight! Everything's dammed up in there."

"Maybe you need to work up to it," Jan says. "Take yourself back to the rowboat. Start there. Let yourself experiment with the idea that it's not all your fault."

The tones trip left to right. I'm shivering under bright sky, feet submerged in biting ocean water. Arthur Fish pivots from the waist, first toward me, then away. Digging and flashing the oars. He's disgusted with me. But what did I do? He knows I wasn't in the boat when it hit the rocks. He's furious anyway. A laughing gull wheels and settles on the bell buoy. It's OK, I tell myself. You didn't make this happen. Your father was one sadistic man. He wanted you to squirm.

My chest opens. Something flies out and feels gone, leaving behind a small, clean space.

"Good," Jan says. "Keep going."

I'm kneeling on the floor of Dad's Mercedes, wheezing for breath, the tang of metal on my tongue. I saw the Pontiac running the light and should've said something. OK, hold on. Rewind the tape. We're stopped at the intersection. We get the green arrow to turn into the parking lot. Dad sees the car coming. We both see the car coming, not slowing for the light. I can hear his stubborn thinking. *You'd better stop. I have the right of way.* He makes the turn, daring the Pontiac to keep coming, swinging my side of the car into its path. If I'd warned him, would he have listened?

I push ahead, panning to the violet dusk beyond the airplane windows. Mom looks over her shoulder at me, an ember-red scar chiseled from temple to chin. The dead left corner of her mouth won't lift. Her eyebrow is a flat line. The tomb-like silence of our house in snow. Slippered invalids haunting the second floor.

"You look like you're in pain," Jan says.

"It's so sad," I whisper, unable to lift my head.

"What's so sad?"

"How long I've been blaming myself. Carrying this horrible weight, wearing it like a necklace that just gets heavier and heavier. I never say, 'Enough! Take it off!'"

"Can you take it off now?"

"I think I let the boat go. And the car crash, too."

"How strong is the feeling in your stomach and chest when you focus on the boat? What number would you give it?"

I close my eyes. "It's almost gone. A two or a three. Same with the car."

"And the plane?"

My stomach knots. I shake my head. The plane is different. That will always be my fault.

"OK. That's all right. You're not completely ready to let go of feeling guilty. But you're well on your way, which is great. So tell yourself that. Tell yourself, 'I'm starting to let go of the blame.'"

She re-sets the tones. I close my eyes. I'm starting to let go of the blame. I breathe deeply. I'm starting to let go. My muscles exhale.

I'm starting.

•

I SIT BY THE fountain in the waiting room. The cat from the upstairs apartment can't resist the sound of running water. She slips in to sit with me. I stroke her and wonder how much longer, how many more times Jan and I will run our routine, heading back to the crash, covering the same ground. She opens the double doors and beckons me in. I head for the couch this time instead of the chair, plopping down in a warm spot left by the last patient. She hands me the headphones.

"Ready?" she asks. "You know what to do."

I peer over Dad's right shoulder. The instrument panel stretches the full width of the cockpit and rises almost to eye level, little rectangles of windshield hung above it like an afterthought. Gauges and dials and knobs glow greener as the dusk deepens. When I slit my eyes, it becomes a cityscape at night. I'm sleepy. I double over, arms crossed on knees, forehead resting on forearms. The engine vibrates through the seats. A cold current finds my legs. I will it away. I'm an idiot for wearing a summer skirt. The trench coat slips off my shoulders as I sit up. I push my face between the front seats and ask for heat. Two hands reach for the panel at once, fingers dipping into its phosphorescence.

My ears pop. My stomach drops into our descent. We're landing. I should sit up, buckle up. It's time, but I can't wake up. Wait! I'm not ready.

Spine jammed against cold metal. I can't turn my head. My eyes dart left and right. There's a green glow on either side. My feet kick somewhere in the dark.

The camera swoops backward for a full view. A cross-section of fuselage is sheered away. I see my whole length from the side, a girl shoehorned into a crumpled tube, her arm erased.

"We're on the ground," I tell Jan. "But now it's like I'm watching myself from the sidelines. There's all the same stuff as before, just smaller. Everything looks further away. What does that mean?"

"What do you think it means?"

"I'm seeing the crash site differently. So, I guess my perspective is changing?"

"That's what it sounds like. Does it feel that way?"

"A little bit."

"All right, keep going. You're on the ground. Everything looks as though it's further away."

I want to do something to help the men get me out, but I'm clamped in place. Only my feet have room. They flutter and scrape in the leaves. There's shouting, then a blast of air against my arm, blood lunging toward my fingertips. A big hand closes over mine. Somehow the capsule expands to receive a stretcher. I want to crawl out on my own. Instead, they strap my head and haul me out feet first. A gasp goes up behind the glare.

"God, that pisses me off," I hiss to Jan.

"What does?"

"The crowd. The spectacle of it. The TV camera aimed at my face, like I'm only there for show. They shouldn't be gawking."

"Why does that bug you so much?"

"I wasn't even hurt. After they freed my arm, there was nothing to see. They loaded me into the ambulance so carefully. A whole crew of them, floating me onboard like I was precious cargo. It was the same ambulance that brought the surgery team to cut off my arm."

"That's intense, Carol. They were about to amputate."

"But they didn't, that's the point. There was so much fuss about getting me out. Surgeons, police, firemen, paramedics, the Jaws of Life. I didn't deserve all that."

"Why not?"

"I had no injuries. I tried to tell them that. They carried me out anyway. I wasn't even hurt."

"You were in a crashed airplane. Your sister was dead. Your parents were seriously injured. They had reason to be careful with you, too."

"I was fine! The whole thing was my fault, anyway. So why bother?"

"Keep going."

Someone crouches beside me in the ambulance, holding a bag of fluid next to my head. It's deep-space quiet. We're sealed inside and gliding over wet streets. I strain to hear the siren. Then it's over. A blaze of overhead lights, the run of metal up my leg. A needle stabbing five, six, seven times. Two doctors and the pastor moving as a unit, stepping close to the exam table. They tell me Dad is in surgery. Mom is in critical condition. Nancy is dead. Cold stealing through the white curtains.

"When they finally figured out I wasn't hurt," I tell Jan, "they didn't know what to do with me."

An empty room on the Children's Ward. They stash me in the bed furthest from the window. Strict hands yank the covers up to my chin and re-tuck the sheets. Buddy, from youth group, pulls a chair close. His whole face is wet. He watches and cries, holding my good hand in both of his. He doesn't try to get me talking. It's OK to be quiet together. I silently study the sheen of tears he doesn't wipe away.

"Nobody else seemed capable of just sitting with me, keeping still," I tell Jan. "They all had to say the crash meant something, served some higher purpose. Or they expected me to say that for them."

"And did you?"

"In the hospital, yes, and even after. I said what they wanted to hear."

"But you didn't believe what you were saying."

"I tried to think of it as an accident. I use that word when I tell the story, but it's not right. It doesn't feel like an accident."

"Because it's still your fault?"

"Nancy died. Mom almost died. Mom said God spared me for some purpose, some great plan."

"Maybe that was her way of dealing with it."

"OK, fine. But as soon as she said it, I knew I'd never get it right. I screw everything up. Why put that on me, after all we'd been through?"

"I want you to try something," Jan says. "Imagine yourself in her hospital room. Go back and see if you can tell her what you're feeling."

Alone at the foot of her bed. A nest of tubes and flashing lights. I want broken bones, gaping wounds like hers. I'm selfish. I want my mother to take care of me.

"I can't say anything! She's lying there with a machine to breathe for her. I shouldn't even touch her. She could still die.

I've already hurt her enough with everything I've done."

"But you know how it turns out. It's safe now. You know she's not going to die."

Silence. "I hadn't thought about it like that."

"You can say what you feel," Jan nudges. "Your words won't kill her. Go back there and talk to her."

The approach to the ICU feels less tentative. I enter her room on my own, walking instead of in a wheelchair. I perch carefully on the bed and reach for her hand. Beneath the swaddling of bandages, the eye patch, the tented sheets, her flesh pulls to attention. She looks at me and the things she is grateful for topple out of her mouth in a hoarse rush. She tells me how glad she is to know that her face, not mine, will carry the scars. A disfigured girl is less likely to marry, she says, but now I still have a chance for that happiness. God has a wonderful plan for my life.

"Mom, please!" I break in. "Don't talk to me about a husband right now. I'm just a kid. Besides, what if I wanted to be scarred? I lived through this, too. Why shouldn't I have something to show for it?"

She is focused on me with both eyes now, the patch gone. She's gripping my hands tightly in hers.

"Where were you?" I ask. "I've been alone and so scared. I couldn't move. You weren't there. You didn't come."

She listens. She sees me. She holds my hands. It occurs to me that the point is not to make her explain. The point is to sit with her differently, to play the scene a new way.

"Everyone expects me to be brave," I tell her. "The way they look at me, they're begging me not to cry. 'Be strong for your mother,' they say. But I don't want to be strong. I want you to pull me close and stroke my head while I bawl. I want your comfort, your touch, your tears. Cry with me. Nothing could be sadder than what has happened to us. Don't make it a sermon or a sign. Just cry with me."

Jan asks what's happening, then waits while I blow my nose.

"It's so much better this way, telling her what I feel instead of swallowing the words." When I hold them inside, it's like a pine cone jammed in my windpipe, brittle and spiky and gummed with sap.

"Good! Let's do it again," she suggests. "What's the image to focus on? What feels best?"

"Sitting beside her on the hospital bed. We're holding hands and crying."

Our tears let loose in the white room. They lap the legs of the tray table and the stiff-backed chair, pooling and rising, dissolving the hard space between us.

"It feels real," I say. "My chest is open, and stuff is whooshing out of me. It feels so much better."

Jan wants me to get more practice saying the things I keep choked in my throat. But I balk when she suggests that writing could help me develop those muscles. I've written about the accident a few times and it always winds up feeling wrong. It seems manipulative and lazy. A writer worth her salt should be able to build drama from something original instead of taking the shortcuts life hands her. Besides, there are other people involved in this story. Writing it down could make them uncomfortable, or worse.

"You're thinking about writing for an audience," she says. "Write for yourself instead. You don't need to show it to anyone."

"Like a journal?" I ask.

"A journal, or maybe a letter you don't have to send. Whatever feels right."

It sounds like one more chore.

"See if you can visualize writing this stuff out of your body. Writing out the things you want to say about the crash."

I close my eyes.

"Get a clear picture with as much detail as you can. Where are you? What does it look like? What does it smell like?"

"I'm at the computer," I say without looking up. "There's a blank file open. The cursor's blinking at the top of the page."

"Good. Use the tones to keep it going."

Nothing much happens at first. The metronome of the tones synchs with the cursor's flashing. I'm wondering how to start, pre-composing an opening line, when I realize my hands are ahead of me, tripping along the keyboard. At first, what spills down the screen is gibberish. Then words start to emerge, and phrases, whole sentences dredged intact from my throat. The torrent of language comes faster than my eye can follow, so I watch my hands instead, a fury of typing. When I swallow, I feel the dam splintering.

"I've broken through," I tell Jan. "I cleared a path."

"A path for what?" she asks.

"I typed and typed until the seal on my throat burst."

"Wow! And nothing bad happened?"

"No, nothing bad. It was such a relief. I could feel this sticky ball of stuff coming apart, high in my chest."

"Is there more? Can you cough it up?"

"I don't know." I pull a few deep breaths through the cleared passage. "I can try."

•

JAN LOOKS UP FROM her notes. "You were starting to tell your mom how you felt after the crash," she reminds me. "Let's do more of that today. Focus on what you've been holding back, what's still unsaid."

I'm at Vi's kitchen table. Dad sits across from me in his plaid bathrobe, arm crooked in a sling, hair fallen limp over his forehead. He wants me to cut it. I tell him I don't know how. He says he doesn't care what it looks like, he just wants the hair out of his eyes. How hard could that be, he asks. I know it's a set-up. But even if I make a mess of it, he'll still get some relief, right? We take the basement stairs haltingly, me in front guiding and bracing. I cover his robe with a plastic cape and try to hold the comb and scissors the way hairdressers do, combing with my left hand and cutting with my right. When I finish he looks in the mirror and wonders aloud how anyone could do such a lousy job.

"I should have refused," I tell Jan. "I should have made him listen."

"At the time you must've felt like you couldn't."

"He was looking for more than a haircut. He's always looking for more."

"You mean when he asked for the haircut it wasn't really

about getting the hair out of his eyes?"

"Right. He was showing me I'm a fuck-up. That I'm less than he is."

"Less capable of cutting hair?"

"He needs to be top dog. He needs proof of it every day. He needs to hear it over and over again in as many ways as I can say it."

"And what do you want to say instead?"

"Go away! Leave me alone."

"Why don't you try?"

I'm with Dad in his Mercedes, heading to the mall. It feels weird to be doing something together, just the two of us, me riding up front. It's quiet. We've run out of things to talk about. I wish I were home, playing cards with Sue in our room. I wish I'd said no when he asked me to come. But I should want to be here. I should want to do things with him. He's my father now. I should be a better daughter. I should love him.

"I can't do it. I can't just tell him to leave me alone. I'm supposed to love him."

"Why?" Jan asks.

"He's my father, that's why. Because Mom loves him."

"Does he love you?"

"He says he does. But it seems like he only says it when he wants something in return."

Bruce and Sue and I are in the living room with Mom. We're digging through a box of old family photographs. We're laughing about the time Aunt Shirley gave the dog an enema. Dad stands in the doorway, arms crossed.

"Your crazy relatives," he says from across the room. "They never approved of me."

Oh, no, we all rush to assure him. Everyone in the family thinks the world of you, Dad.

"He inserts himself into everything," I tell Jan. "He needs constant attention, constant praise. Everyone has to agree that he's the best. If I'm bad at something, he keeps bringing it up. If I'm good at something, he has to be better."

"And your mother? What does she say about all this competition?"

"I get this image of her nudging me forward. Shooing me toward him."

"What for?"

"To show him I'm grateful. To thank him."

"Thank him for what?"

"Anything and everything. For taking us out to dinner. Paying for new school shoes. She doesn't say it, but I know I'm supposed to love him for taking care of me. Tell him he's the best Daddy ever."

"And that's not what you want to do."

"She's always expecting me to reassure him about something, but I can't figure out what because it keeps changing. A good daughter would know what to do. A good daughter would meet her father's needs, fulfill his wishes even before he asks."

"Stay with that," she tells me, firing the tones.

Afternoon light dissolving on the lawn, retreating to the edge of the woods behind Al and Vi's house. I'm sitting with Dad again because he needs to talk. He doesn't ask if I'm OK to listen. He runs through the final approach sequence as he remembers it. Sighting the outer marker. The tower granting clearance for landing. A bank of lights below to port. Then struggling to come to in the baggage hold. Urging Mom out. Telling me to move my feet. His voice, flat and trance-like, brings the dark keening back.

"You saved my life," he announces, breaking the spell.

I'm back in the bright kitchen and can't scrape my eyes off his face. He says he would have killed himself if he thought the crash was his fault. Now we know it was the carbon monoxide. No one with that much poison in his system could have remained conscious. He held on until the very last minute. I told the doctors I couldn't wake up for landing. He says that saved his life.

"I don't want it," I blurt to Jan, swiping the headset away.

"Don't want what?" she asks. "What's happening?"

"I didn't save his life! He would never have killed himself. No way. I don't know why he'd say that, except to get something out of me. But I never know what it is he wants, and I'm sick of trying to guess. That's not my job!"

"You're right. It's not."

"I can't keep groping in the dark for ways to please him. If there's something he needs from me, let him ask for it."

"Yes! Go with that."

Christmastime. New England postcard winter. I'm trying to light a fire in my parents' family room, but the chimney is cold. Smoke backs up into the room. Matteo pantomimes a slow, wheezing death, then moves to the kitchen to finish reading the sports section. Tomorrow we fly back to San Francisco. Tonight Mom wants everyone in the family room for a conference. Dad purses his lips and pushes out a long, loud exhale.

"Are you sure that's a good idea?" he whines. "Those don't go so well."

He's referring, of course, to the time he confessed that he'd rather I died and Nancy survived. He reminds us once again how hard on him that confession was. His pain is still fresh. I'm holding a flaming wad of newspaper up the flue to draw the smoke. I drop it into the grate and tell him what I now realize about that day. It was brave of him to say what he did. It took guts to be so honest.

"Hold on. You thought that was brave?" Jan asks. "Saying he wished you'd been killed?"

"It can't have been easy to tell the truth, but he did. Now that I'm older, I see it was admirable of him to be honest."

"Admirable? Really? You think so?"

"The thing is, it wasn't enough to just say once that he was brave. He keeps making me repeat it. Whenever we try to have a serious family discussion, he'll make a big fuss about getting into hot water for speaking up that time. Then I'll have to re-mind him all over again that I admire his honesty. It's like he's testing my credibility, pushing to see if I really mean it."

"Why do you think he has doubts about that?"

"Maybe because he says things he doesn't really believe, so he thinks I'm doing the same."

"Like what?"

"Like telling me I saved his life. He couldn't really believe that. It's so ludicrous. He must've been grasping at anything to make the facts tolerable. If he pretended I was spared to save his life, maybe he could stand that I lived and Nancy died."

"That's really convoluted, Carol. You're saying your dad dealt with the fact that you lived and Nancy died by telling himself you had to live in order to save his life?"

"Possibly."

"Like the way your mom said there was some great purpose in store for you."

"Except my mom actually believes that."

Jan pauses, tapping her pen against her pad. "And you still think it was courageous of him to tell you he wished you died instead of Nancy?"

"Maybe not courageous. But at least it was the truth."

It's the one message he never masks. I hear it all the time, loud and clear. I saved his life, but he wouldn't have saved mine.

·

THERE'S A BLACK-AND-WHITE photo, a Polaroid of Bruce, Sue, Nancy and me taken on Christmas Eve. We're at Dad's house. He and Mom aren't married yet. She's in the kitchen finishing up the dishes from supper. Before Dad takes our picture, he gathers us on the living room floor at his feet. He's perched on the arm of the sofa. He leans in and stage-whispers that he and Mom want to get married so they can be Mom and Dad to all four of us together. We'll be one family. But first they need our permission, he says. I know he means right now, not in a few days or weeks, after we've had time to talk it over. I also know he isn't really asking for permission. The marriage will happen no matter what we say. Still, my belly clenches at the responsibility. My eyes dart between Bruce and Sue. I need to know what they're thinking, but neither meets my gaze. First one hand goes up in silent approval, then a second and a third until I'm the only holdout. I shoot mine up quickly to cover my hesitation.

Satisfied with the vote, Dad poses us in front of the fireplace, telling us to scrunch in close. Nancy sits cross-legged in her nightgown, a hammock of fabric slung between splayed knees. Sue and Bruce reach to press it down, trying to keep her underpants from showing in the photo. I look into the camera with a glassy-eyed grin that hides my slow, unscrolling panic.

I do not want a new father. Things have been nice for Mom and Bruce and Sue and me with our first father gone. I do not want a little sister. I'm supposed to be the youngest, the one Mom calls baby. I do not want to leave my teacher, Mrs. Campo, or my desk between Tommy and Michelle, or our house on the street where my best friend and I ride our matching banana-seat bikes.

But I've already lost these things. I've lost Mom to this picture of a new family, a new life with a purple Mercedes and a red riding lawnmower and acres of green grass. I see the way her face flushes and hear her voice dart up to a high, breathless place when she talks about Dad. It happens during our long drives to his office in Massachusetts, just Mom and me. We go there so he can give me a shot or crack my bones while I lie on a padded table that he pumps up and down with his foot. Mom lies on the table after me to have her bones cracked, too, while I play Barbies in the waiting room. When I am not watching her face in the car, I watch the shoulder of the road so I can point out how the pavement turns from gray to reddish-purple when we cross the state line. She says, "Uh-huh," but doesn't look. Back home in our kitchen in Maine, she opens the mail and bends double laughing at something in her hand. She holds it out for me to see. It's a small square of paper with a name and address and telephone number at the top in block lettering. Someone has used magic marker to write "bills, bills, bills, bills, bills" down the page. I don't see what's funny. She explains that she asked Dad to please send her a bill for cracking our bones and this piece of paper was his reply. "He's saying we don't have to pay!" she trills in that high, winded voice.

"You didn't want to compete with this new guy for your mom's attention," Jan says. "You were how old?"

"Seven, almost eight."

"Little. You didn't want to share your mom. That's normal."

"It might have been normal, but that doesn't make me feel any less guilty. I was supposed to be happy with the situation. I was definitely not happy, but I couldn't say so. Everyone else seemed in favor of it. I should've been in favor of it, too."

"Go with that."

No. No! I don't want it. No new house. No new school. No new father. Definitely no new sister. Her first birthday with us, Bruce and Sue help her blow out the candles, fussing over her like I'm not even there. She falls off her bike and acts like it's an emergency. Mom scoops her up, hugs her close for every little scrape. At her memorial service we sing the hymn "We Gather Together." Someone claims it was her favorite. No it wasn't.

"People made all this stuff up about Nancy after she died, as if she'd been some perfect little girl," I tell Jan. "I really hated that."

"What did you hate about it?"

"It was like anybody could say anything they wanted about her, as long as it was good." But I knew the truth. She poked and provoked incessantly. Mom said it was because she wanted my attention. She looked up to her big sister. And it was my job to set a good example. But when Nancy pulled that crap, all I wanted to do was hurt her badly enough to make it stop. She had this fake laugh. If she kept it up long enough, it turned into a real laugh that I couldn't shake out of her. But I couldn't resist joining in, either. I hated being pulled into that laughter.

"You sound really angry."

"You're right, I shouldn't be."

"I didn't say you shouldn't be. But is that how you feel? Like you're not allowed to be angry with Nancy?"

"She had a really hard start in life." During Dad's divorce she was shunted from one baby sitter to the next. Before that there were diaper pins and slaps from the lady with the black VW. When the rest of us talked about our old life in Maine she always wanted to know, "Who took care of me?" Nobody, as far as I could tell. I tried to keep this in mind whenever I wanted to kill her.

"Instead of showing your anger in some way," Jan says, "you felt you had to suck it up and be good, even when she was provoking you."

I met a girl at camp the summer after eighth grade. We were in the same cabin and fell hard for one another, almost instantly, like two halves of a self. She reminded me of Nancy physically, and in lots of other ways. She shadowed me and planted herself at the center of my attention. I welcomed it, even though she would spin into nasty moods and do and say horrible things to the other girls. I intervened on her behalf every time, making excuses and apologies. When she finally turned on me with bared fangs, I went into the woods, snapped a sharp stick off a pine branch and dug so many bloody gouges in my bare legs I lost count at fifty.

"I guess I was always sucking it up," I tell Jan. "Playing the model older sister, the martyr, the one who just takes it and takes it."

"And then takes it out on herself when she can't take it out on whoever she's really mad at. Like the girl at camp, or Nancy."

Or Dad. Or Mom. Or Matteo.

"Try this. Get in touch right now with that feeling of being really angry with Nancy. What would happen if you showed your true colors, if you let some of your anger out instead of short-circuiting it?"

She turns on the tones. I'm in the plane, swatting Nancy away. Get off! Leave me alone! Then she's in her white casket, body hard as cement. Her stillness is a relief.

"Part of me was grateful that she'd finally stopped harassing me," I confess quietly.

Jan says, "You know, just wishing someone away doesn't make it happen. We wish things all the time."

"But she was my sister. It was wrong to wish that."

"I'm curious about something. Say things were different the day of the crash. Say you were happy to be with her on the plane. Because sometimes you were, right?"

"When she wasn't being a pain."

"So imagine this is one of those times when you're getting along. Bring that feeling on to the plane and see what happens."

Purple dusk deepens quickly to dark outside my window. I watch the red light on the wing flash into the murk until my eyelids droop. I shift lower in the seat and close my eyes. Nancy pokes me in the side. She's just bored. "I'm going to sleep now," I tell her calmly. "What are you going to do?" At first she hesitates, hand poised for another jab. Then she shrugs and picks up her book, bringing it so close to her face that her nose almost touches the page. I pull my coat over my head to block out the cabin light and fold over to sleep. Muffled voices in the dark. A Boston accent asks my name, where I live, what day this is. Two doctors in white coats lean over my bed to tell me Nancy's dead.

"I guess it doesn't matter that I got mad and slapped her," I tell Jan. "I just replayed it being nice. She still would've died."

"All right. Go with that."

She slows the tones. Nancy turns to face me. We're sitting side by side in the grass, resting. It's hot and her glasses have slid down her nose. We've been practicing for a backyard gymnastics show all afternoon. I spot her while she takes long tumbling runs, doing handsprings and flips. She's winded but giddy, wiggling her eyebrows, mouth lifted in a goofy, buck-toothed grin. I study her face, breathe with the tones and feed words down the channels of my body. When she let me, I was a good sister. She didn't make it easy, but sometimes I found a way to love her. As I repeat these things to myself, something lets go in my neck and shoulders. I loved her enough. I did the best I could.

·

JAN ASKS ME WHAT I'd like to change about myself and my life going forward. I answer without hesitation.

"Number one," I tell her, "I want to know what I want. Instead of always worrying about what everyone else wants."

"Great," she says. "Once you figure that out, then what?"

"I want to speak up. I want to believe it's not wrong to ask for the things that make me happy and healthy."

"Good."

"And I want to feel wanted. Loved. I want to know that I deserve to be loved, maybe even adored once in a while."

"Now you're pushing it," she deadpans.

I giggle.

"So where should we start?"

"With work. I need to figure out what I want to do with myself. I need to find a new career."

"Something creative, I assume."

"Definitely. But I can't support myself on poetry. The things I'm good at aren't worth much. Mom says she doesn't know where her kids get their talent. It's supposed to be a compliment, but I get the feeling she mostly worries about us making ends meet."

"So let me ask you this. When you imagine following your own voice and doing something creative professionally, does it make you feel like you're breaking some bond with your mom? Like you should always be united in everything?"

"Yeah," I tell her, tearing up. "I have to do what she needs me to do. It's like a wedge forced down my throat, scraping up my insides. But now that I've said it, my body wants to let it fly."

"Why don't you?"

"I don't know. I'm supposed to be with my parents, not against them. If I stand apart, if I'm different, that's the same as not participating. That's not OK."

"I can see why you're so angry with them," Jan says.

"What's that supposed to mean?"

"You just want to be yourself, right? But sometimes that's not OK with them. When you sense their disapproval, you feel bad. So you drop it. That would piss anybody off."

"Sometimes I wonder if I even know what anger is," I tell her.

"Can you remember a time when you actually got angry with them?"

"Maybe during those lectures. I had to sit in the rocking chair and listen to Dad's catalog of what's wrong with me."

"OK, good," she says.

"But I was screwing up, skipping school, throwing parties. I smashed up the car."

"So?"

"I deserved the speech. I don't get to be angry at them for

EVERY MOMENT OF A FALL

that."

"I want you to try something for me," she says. "Try visualizing whatever it is that's keeping your anger away, whatever's separating you from those feelings."

I'm standing so close to a wall I feel my breath bounce off its surface. When I tilt my head and look up, there's only a scrap of sky the wall hasn't blotted out. I step back. From a few feet away I see it's not exactly a wall. More like the door to a vault. A towering steel slab as thick as my forearm.

"It's a door," I report to Jan. "An enormous steel door."

"Give me some dimensions."

"When I stood right next to it and looked up, I could barely see the sky."

"That's big," she agrees. "Can you try to get through it?"

"I don't think so. I'm not strong enough."

"Give it a try. Focus on what you need to get through it."

The door looms, defying me. It stretches in all directions. I drop my head, defeated. I can't do it. I'm staring daggers at my feet when I notice how green the grass is. Grass? It's growing everywhere, acres of it, the juicy, deep-green color of June. Where the grass ends, blue sky begins, lazy with the slow passing of clouds.

"It's still a big, heavy door, but now there's lots of space around the frame. It's standing in a wide-open field."

"Perfect. Can you take a peek around it before you go through, just to see what's on the other side?"

My palms are clammy. I'm up against the door, one hot cheek pressed to its metal. All the strength has funneled out of me. Taking a step feels like dragging an anvil through gravel. I have no idea what's waiting on the other side, but whatever it is has filed its claws in anticipation. I force myself, inch by inch, along the steel surface to its edge. Then I squeeze my eyes shut, count to three and fling myself forward.

They're all there. Matteo, my parents, my brothers and sister. All waiting in the sunshine. When they see me round the corner, they whoop and clap, cheering me forward. Matteo smiles and pumps his fist. He's wearing his blue polo shirt and plaid Bermuda shorts. I haven't seen him in that outfit for years. Mom kisses me and we both start to cry. She tells me that she loves me. She's hugging me so tight her words buzz against my chest.

Jan cuts the tones and asks, "Why the tears?"

"It was the hardest thing. At first, I couldn't even make myself move. But when I came around the corner, everyone was there. And they were happy for me. It felt completely real, like it was all happening, clear as day."

She wants me to do it again.

This time I don't linger on the lonely side of the door. I give it a little kick and then trot around to join the others. They're all still there, applauding. They actually brighten when they see me. They like having me around. Jan lets the tones play. Bruce and Sue and Mom come close. I scan the crowd for Matteo but he's drifted away. After his initial enthusiasm, he lost interest.

"Maybe that's one of the things I'm angry about," I tell Jan. "Certain people perk up around me. I see it in the visualization, and I know it's there in real life, too. They're happy to see me. They want me close, especially Mom, Bruce and Sue."

"What makes you angry about that?"

"Nothing. It's just so obviously not the same for Matteo. He doesn't light up when I walk into a room. His eyes don't follow me. He doesn't pull me close. He barely notices I'm there."

"And that's making you angry."

"He keeps me at arm's length. He doesn't see me. He doesn't desire me. It doesn't seem like he wants me in his life."

"What are you feeling right now as you're saying this?"

"I'm not sure. It pisses me off, but that fizzles out pretty fast. I wind up just feeling sad."

"Let's try the exercise again. This time, though, find a way to make contact with those feelings."

I'm alone in the cold shadow. Everyone I love is on the other side. "How dare you!" I scream. "Don't just stand there. Get the hell out of my way!" I ram the door with my boot sole, battering the surface until I'm winded. I lean in and start slapping with the flat of my palm. There's a seam down the middle. Now I see it's really two doors, two huge panels like an elevator. I jam one hand into the crease, then the other, and feel something give. I pry open a breach wide enough to kick my boot in and wedge myself between the two panels. I give the doors a final shove. All my people are on the other side, surprised and excited that I've managed to break through. They whistle and clap.

"That time I got really pissed!" I tell Jan. "I kicked and clawed and pried the doors open. Boy did that feel good."

"What do you think it means? Why did it help to go through instead of around?"

"Going around felt like avoiding, like I was a scared little kid sneaking around. When I went straight through, I was an adult. An angry adult. I felt powerful."

"Good. Great! So go back and take the direct route again. See what you do with your anger when you get there."

He won't look at me, filling the wrenched-open doorway. Drinks and secret calls with a woman from work. That's what he's been up to for the better part of a year, maybe longer. Hours on the phone in the middle of the night. Convincing me to move out. Reeling me in for a weekend, then throwing me back. Sometimes he tells me to my face that he doesn't want me, that he needs to fuck around. Mostly he evades, denying the intimacy of those late-night calls and furtive meetings in bars. Saying they're just friends.

"What a crock of shit!" I spit out. "I can't believe what he's done to our relationship."

"What has he done?"

"He knew I didn't want it to end. He said he wasn't sure. He saw me fighting for it, but went ahead with all his sordid bullshit anyway. When I pushed back, he acted like he wanted to fight for us, too. But he's still holding out, still treating me like an acquaintance."

"You're angry?"

"Hell yeah, I'm angry! He agrees to go to couples therapy with me, then he takes off to Italy for months? OK, so it's a good opportunity for him. I should be supportive. Fine. Meanwhile, you and I do all this work together and I'm excited about the changes I see in myself. I can't wait to share them with him. Now he comes back and says he doesn't believe anything's different."

"When did he say that?"

"In our couples session. I brought a fucking list of my accomplishments to prove how productive I'd been while he was away. He made some snide comment about me being a list maker. Said that if I'd really wanted to find a job or a publisher for my manuscript, I'd have already done it. Not just taken steps."

"Hmm."

"He said nothing on my list was just for him. How twisted is that? All the ways I'm doing better and feeling better benefit him, too. If I'm no longer a black heap on the couch, if every day I feel more and more alive, that's great news for both of us. But he just rolls over in bed and turns his back."

Jan says, "Now you really sound angry."

"I hate reporting to him this way. Like I have to prove I'm good enough. What do I have to do to deserve a hug? He wants something more from me. Something I should be doing. What is it? What does he want?"

"That sounds familiar," Jan says. "Like trying to figure out what your dad really wants."

"Oh that's just fucking great! More stuff I have to get angry about. What am I supposed to do with all of it?"

"Take one thing at a time. Let's stay with Matteo for now. Picture yourself talking with him. You're lying in bed. He's turned his back to you. What do you want to do? What do you want to say?"

I'm sitting up, knees hugged to my chest, tenting my half of the covers. The heat coming off of him has a taste. It's bitter, like putting your fingers to your lips after pulling weeds. But I ask him to turn over, and he does. I tell him there are things I need to say. He doesn't roll his eyes or flop down on the pillow groaning. He looks at me. I tell him how lonesome it feels to be constantly pushed away. I tell him I want to be wanted and desired, not reminded over and over that I am defective, un-lovely, a drudge. When I try to say how angry it makes me to be treated this way, to be deceived and dismissed, the feelings don't hold together. They pixilate and crumble before I can put them into words.

"Well, at least I was able to say something," I tell Jan. "I made him look at me and listen. But it feels like stuff is still stuck in my throat."

She asks, "Are you keeping it there deliberately? Holding it back?"

I must be.

"Time to go have a look," she tells me. "Go see what's stuck in there."

•

IT DOESN'T OCCUR TO me to ask how she expects me to look down my throat. I just do it. The tones pong left to right and I'm crouching in darkness, ducking my head into the mouth of a cave. It's too dark to make out the contours of the space, but the play of air on my face suggests an opening ahead. I creep forward on all fours until I come to a place where the tunnel floor falls away. A current of air wafts out of this deep. I stand

and let my eyes adjust. Three blackbirds slowly surface in the dark. They drift close over my head, then rise. I see myself in profile as one after another the birds shoot out of my mouth and flap away.

I gasp. Jan cuts the tones.

"I get the feeling there are lots more down there," I tell her. "But I can't see much. It's too dark."

"So get a flashlight and take another look."

I aim the light a few paces ahead and follow it to the edge where the floor of the cave drops away. I point the beam down, sweeping it slowly through the dark. It's a pit, maybe thirty feet deep, with sheer walls broken up by dozens of narrow ledges and outcroppings. Each of these surfaces is packed with roosting birds. As I move my light over them, I see they're not black after all, but white, maybe doves. They begin to stir, feathers riffling, necks bobbing. Some rise to their feet. Then, in a whistling burst, they're aloft. Hundreds of beating wings. The air clots with feathers like furred snowflakes. When it clears, I look up. My mouth is an "O" like the opening of a smoke stack. The birds fly in spirals high above me. They slowly disappear through the bright hole like a train pulled through the moon. The cave walls around me relax.

"They're gone."

"Good," she says. "Now go look again. Make sure everything's cleared out."

I lie flat on my stomach and hang my head over the edge, into the pit. I snap on the flashlight. Its beam slices the stillness. My elbow brushes bits of gravel that ricochet down the rock face, echoing. I sweep the light over the walls. The yawning space seems empty. I'm searching the cavern floor, making sure, when the beam catches a pair of bare feet. I freeze for a moment, then train the light up ankles and shins, to arms and a head. It's a girl. Hunched over, hugging her knees in the dark at the bottom of my throat. Waves of streaky blond hair spill over her shoulders. If I lean down and stretch my arm as far as it can reach, I'll be able to grab her hand. I call to her.

When she looks up, I recognize her from the Polaroid. She's the girl gazing into the camera on Christmas Eve. The man snapping the picture is about to become her father, and there's nothing she can do about it.

She's me. And she's alone.

•

"THOSE WERE SOME INCREDIBLE visualizations," Jan says flipping through a sheaf of notes from our last session.

"Isn't it like that for everyone?" I ask.

"I wish!" she laughs. "People don't usually see birds flying out of their mouths or little girls stuck in their throats."

I stiffen. Maybe I'm some kind of nut job.

"Relax," she says. "You're doing exactly what you need to. Just go with it. Strange, amazing, whatever. The things you're seeing feel true, right?"

"Completely."

"That's what matters. You're a visual person. I'm the same way. It makes sense that images play a central role in your process." She's looking me in the face like she means it.

"How do you feel today?" she asks.

I swallow. "Better," I say. "There's more space inside of me. I wonder if this is how clear my throat and chest are supposed to be."

"What about the girl? Is she still down there?"

"I'm not sure."

"Why not go and see."

Dark. Damp. I cross my arms tight over my chest and hunch there, waiting. Slowly the dark becomes a little less solid. Motes of light swim past and settle at my feet. I crane my neck to see where they're coming from, but the source is somewhere high above. The glow they give off is enough to make out the contours of the tunnel, its sweating walls. I sink into the al-most-dark and listen. My skin prickles. There's a presence. Not a voice, not even the sound of breath. Just a whiff of something with me.

"Is someone here?" I call out.

No response. I ask again, and this time there's a scraping of feet in the tunnel ahead of me. She shuffles into the half light where I can see her.

"It's time to get out of here," I tell her.

I hold out a hand. She reaches for it, but something has her by the legs. I move closer, grasp both of her hands in mine and heave for all I'm worth. When she tumbles out of my mouth, a rush of fluid comes splattering after her.

"What a weirdly perfect image," I tell Jan. "Afterbirth. Like maybe I'm getting another chance."

"You're giving yourself another chance. Let's make sure there's nothing still down there blocking your way."

There's more light now. I can see that the cave is empty. I coax myself forward, poking into corners to be certain.

"All clear," I tell Jan when she stops the tones.

"Good," she says. "And the little girl you found down there is where, now?"

"I don't know. She must be somewhere around here."

"See if you can find her. Maybe she can tell you how she got trapped in the first place."

We're in a blank room. Nothing but white walls. She's wearing the blue bathrobe Mom made for her: floor length, with a white organza ruffle. She draws her knees to her chest, tugs the robe closed and looks up, blinking.

"What were you doing down there?" I ask her.

She shrugs and says she stumbled and fell. She tried to climb out but couldn't manage it on her own. For a long time she called for help. No one heard. No one came. So she gave up. Then things started falling down my throat and landing on top of her. Things that hurt or made her angry. They were black and sticky like tar. She slapped them into a ball of goo. The ball grew and grew until it got so big it rolled over her legs and pinned her beneath it.

"OK," Jan says, nodding. "OK. So when things happened that made you sad or angry, and when you couldn't say anything or do anything to make it better, it was like being stuck in tar. And the tar got thicker and thicker the more it happened until you felt totally trapped. Is that it?"

I see the girl kneeling in the dark, eyes wide. Dose after dose of black sludge splattering down.

I'm twenty-three, naked on all fours. There's the slap of skin on skin and my boyfriend's British accent saying, "Look how fat you are! It's disgusting!"

I'm seventeen, standing in Dad's exam room willing myself to disappear. I concentrate on the pattern in the rug while he talks about me to a colleague. "Notice the classic way she carries her weight below the waist," Dad says. "She's storing fat reserves for childbearing." He tells me to lift my T-shirt a bit so they can study my abdomen. The other doctor teases me about a piece of lint peeking out of my belly button. Dad hits the roof. "Why aren't you washing yourself properly?" he demands. "I didn't raise you to be a slob!"

I'm twelve. It's family weekend at a Baptist revival camp. The preacher's family leads us in gospel songs by the campfire. When the singing is done, the sermon begins. The preacher calls us liars, cheaters, filthy sinners. Damned to hell unless we repent. I feel the flames in my cheeks. He's trying to terrify us into salvation. Mom notices my tears and approves. She thinks I'm sorry for my sins. It's not guilt I'm feeling, though. It's rage at being bullied into submission. Belittled. Smashed down over and over again. But I can't tell her that.

Jan asks why I'm crying. I describe the hail of dark memories. Times I was humiliated. Times I couldn't fight back. It's all down there, gummed together in a big ball of tar.

"You need to get that ball out," she says.

"How am I supposed to do that?" She doesn't know how much this stuff hurts.

"Maybe you can grow yourself up. Let the girl become an adult so she can help."

I close my eyes in refusal. I'm sick of this psychological scavenger hunt. It's too bloody hard. But I can't give up now. I want all that gunk out of my chest. I'll never get anywhere dragging it around.

I take a slow breath and let the tones color in the blue of the girl's robe against her yellow hair. I tell her we have to go back down my throat to get the black ball. But first, I need her to grow up to adult size. Then maybe we'll be able to roll the sticky mess out of there together. She nods and squeezes her eyes shut. I step back, giving her space, and watch my eight-year-old self stretch to occupy a six-foot frame.

The woman standing before me is different from the one I saw this morning in the bathroom mirror. She is tall and smart and strong. She's desirable and capable and whole.

I lead her back through the cave of my mouth. We crab-walk to the place where my trachea falls away like a chute, and dangle our legs into the empty space. Then we let ourselves drop through the dark. It's not nearly as deep as I'd remembered. The tar ball rests heavily against the spongy wall of my throat. Shoulder height, it looks solid as a boulder. But with the strength of four arms it's easy to roll it back through the tunnel. We heave the ball over the ledge. It bounces gently on my tongue while we hoist ourselves up. Then, with a running start, we boot the black mess out of my mouth.

"Good work," Jan says. She wants me to be certain it's gone, totally destroyed.

I replay a video of the black clump shooting out of my mouth in stop motion. My head in profile fills the screen. The sticky mass launches out, frame by frame, and explodes inches from my face. Disintegrated to black flecks in a gray poof.

"OK, it's definitely gone," I tell her. "I blew it up."

"What's it like in there now?"

The other me is missing. Or maybe we're stitched inside the same skin now. The space around me has changed so much that I like being here. I plant my feet in my stomach and gaze out the porthole of my mouth. I'm standing in a stone tower, filling it from floor to ceiling. It's empty, but nothing about the emptiness feels sad. It's what I need. Huge, arched windows at the top are flung open to the air. I can see out in every direction. Wind eddies around me like warm, clean breath.

•

A FRIEND HAS BEEN out of work since the dot-com bubble burst. She tells me about the workshop she attended for people making career transitions. As she describes the exercises the group did together, the hopefulness she feels is palpable. That's what I need if I'm going to figure out how to make my livelihood from something that sustains me. So I sign up.

The workshop leader emails an assignment to complete before the first meeting. I have to ask five people who know me well what adjectives they'd use to characterize me. When I compile my friends' and family's responses, the list is so astonishing I burst into tears. Bold, they call me. And capable, brilliant, inspiring, beautiful, clever, insightful, creative, fierce.

When I ask Matteo the same question, the words he comes up with to describe me are smart, friendly and pretty. I laugh because I think he's kidding, making fun of the exercise. But he's serious. To him, nothing about me is superlative. Where the others used expansive language, he draws three tight circles. I shrink from brilliant to smart, fierce to friendly, beautiful to pretty. I try to tell myself that, after fifteen years together, his words are good enough.

The first day of the workshop, we spend hours reviewing our lives, pinpointing the moments we felt most creative and satisfied. When it comes time to share the personal timelines we've made, I panic. Glancing at what the women on either side of me are ready to present, I realize I've done mine wrong. They organized their life events chronologically in neat columns, while I randomly filled the page with doodles, stickers, colored pencil drawings and a scattering of words. I begin my presentation calling attention to this, making a cutting quip to paper over my embarrassment. Later that evening, as I'm taking stock of the session, I can hear both Connie and Jan chastising me. You were trying to do it perfectly when there was no right way. You did it differently from the others. So what? You are different. That's a good thing.

The second day of the workshop, we talk about the transition from one career to another. Our facilitator says that grief is an essential part of the process. If we don't acknowledge the end of something, we can't fully enter into whatever's next. This idea needles me for the rest of the day. As we move on to other topics, I keep circling back to grief. What's stopping me from getting closure on my academic career? I know I'll never be a tenured professor, but it's hard to let that go after all the work I've done.

During the closing group discussion, a woman named Helen tells me, "Every time you talk, all I keep thinking is, 'She's a writer.'" Heads nod in agreement. Instead of ducking it, I let the remark sink in. She's right. I am a writer. I've worked as a teacher, a waitress, an academic administrator. I've scooped ice cream, cleaned houses, answered phones. But I haven't figured out how to make a career of what I do best. I need to find a way to get paid for my writing.

·

"HOW SHOULD WE DO this?" Jan asks.

"I don't know," I answer. "I guess I imagined it kind of like a funeral."

"So try that," she suggests. "See what happens."

I close my eyes. I'm standing, head bowed, over a freshly filled grave. There's no inscription on the headstone, but I don't need one. My teaching career is buried here. I watch and wait for the tones to summon the next scene, but the picture stalls, stilled in black and white.

"I'm standing at a grave. I want to move things along but I can't. Something still feels unfinished."

"How about adding words?" she offers. "What would you say?"

"Something like, 'My time in academia is over. It's OK to close that chapter.'"

"So go with that."

I'm in a dim corridor. The open door at the far end is a postage stamp of sunshine. Dozens of other doors, each one closed and locked, line the hallway between me and that bright exit. The corridor smells of floor wax and scalded coffee. This could be almost any institutional setting anywhere. But I know exactly where I am.

"I'm in the building where I taught my last college classes," I tell Jan.

"What are you going to do?" she wants to know.

"I have to get out that door."

If only the soles of my shoes weren't bolted to the floor. It feels like the anger door all over again. I pry my feet loose and inch forward, grunting and swearing toward the exit. Just before I reach it, the door slams shut. I lean my full weight into the metal bar and stumble out onto a landing. Sunshine slams me full in the face, so blinding I wince. In the dim of Jan's office, with the shades drawn, my body responds as if a car has blasted its high beams against my eyelids.

"You actually saw a light?" she asks.

"Saw it. Felt it blazing against my face. My pupils contracted. I thought you'd done something."

"Such as?"

"Switched on all the lights, maybe. Or pointed a flashlight at me."

She glances from one hand to the other, then back at me. No flashlight. She smiles. "I can't wait to find out what's next."

I pause on the landing in the sunshine. My shoulders go liquid.

I laugh out loud. And then it's time to shut the door. I throw a hip against it to be certain it latches. There is no handle on this side, no way to get back in. That's a relief. A paved lane materializes at my feet. It cuts through campus and I follow, glancing back periodically to make sure the door stays closed. Each time I look back it's smaller, until I can pinch it between my thumb and index finger. The way forward winds through sunshine and rolling green. Cresting a comically round hill, I spot something in the path ahead. It's a desk, strewn with notebooks and papers. I sit down, scoot the chair in close and consider the view. Tall grass ripples to the horizon. Acres of light and sky. A writer's view, nothing to break my concentration. I sweep the clutter of papers to the ground in one clean pass. A laptop appears in the center of the desk. I flip it open and begin to type.

Several days later I'm home at my desk in the early morning. I watch as my neighbor adds one more row of cinder blocks to the terrace he's slowly carving into the slope of his yard. I'm reworking a poem on my laptop. The one that moves from rowboat to car accident to plane crash. I play with new phrasing, shuffle line breaks and test end rhymes, struggling to describe the moment the firemen sprung me from the fuselage. I type, "Pulled by my feet into light," and the poem pivots suddenly like a fast flock of birds. Surviving the crash becomes a resurrection, a deliverance. The poem's final line, "Where's the harm in living?" is no longer a whimpered apology. It's an invitation. Maybe Dad didn't welcome me back into the world, but I don't need his permission any more to live my life. I'm learning to give myself permission. I hit save, close the file and turn to something new.

•

"YOU CAN COME BACK whenever you want," Jan assures me. "Just call."

I nod. She and I have reached what feels like a natural stopping point, at least for now. The urgency for regular EMDR sessions has passed. And I've still got my weekly slot with Connie.

"So what do you want to end with?" she asks. "How should we conclude?"

"I still need some help staying productive. I'm not working hard enough."

"What makes you think that?"

"I wasted so much time when we first moved to California." I spent at least a year sitting around doing nothing. I should have been planning, strategizing, networking. Month after month went by and I couldn't force myself off the couch. "I'll never make up for all that lost time."

"Why do you have to make up for it?"

"I've pissed away so much of my life. I could work non-stop from now on and never catch up."

"Catching up isn't the point. Living your life is. And part of living, for all of us, is taking breaks. It's how we stay productive."

"I'm afraid if I take a break I'll slip back into doing nothing. I'm worthless if I'm not doing my part, working constantly."

"When you say that, what image comes up?"

"I'm in the living room of our house. Here in San Francisco."

"Describe it for me. What's going on?"

It's afternoon. The sun is low in the sky, cutting sharply through the picture window. I'm sitting on the couch, just staring. I don't get up to draw the blinds. There's no sound. No voices, no traffic, no music. I'm wearing baggy sweats and a huge T-shirt.

"What are you feeling?"

"Numb. Cut off. Everything's muffled, like I'm wrapped in layers of padding."

"OK, good. Stay with that." She hands me the headset.

I close my eyes and listen left, right, left. The heaviness pins me in place.

"What are you feeling now?" she asks.

"Sadness. More than that, desolation. I feel bereft."

"Where in your body do you feel it?"

"My chest is so tight. I have to concentrate to breathe. Every part of me feels too heavy to lift. Even my eyelashes."

"What happens when you try thinking something like, 'It's OK to rest,' while you're picturing yourself there?"

She presses play. I'm willing to concede that I do, in fact, work hard at a handful of things. The administrative job I've taken at the art college. The garden I've wrested from the jungle in our backyard. And it makes sense, objectively, that rest has to balance work. But my stomach doesn't buy it. Each time the new belief tries to find a footing, my gut flutters higher in my throat. Enough will never be enough.

"I can't," I tell her. "It won't take. I've been comatose for too long. There's so much dead time, so much nothing to make up for. But I don't even have the energy to open my eyes. I'm afraid of what I'll see."

"Which is what?"

I can't answer.

"Try this. Picture a heavy curtain. Get it clear in your mind. The color, the weight, the smell of it."

Blue-black velvet. A five-inch hem of lint where it slides along the floor.

"Whatever's behind the curtain is what you're afraid to see," she explains. "So now I want you to look. Just look. You don't have to do anything except get past that curtain."

I'm up against the fabric, breathing its dust. My hand finds an opening. I hold my breath and slide through into pitch darkness. I straighten, still clutching a fistful of velvet. What's here with me? What's waiting to pounce? I pick out a dim cluster of lights glowing faintly green and move toward it. The glow is coming off a console of gauges and dials and switches casting their own phantom moonlight. I stand over what's left of the airplane cockpit, peering down at my pinned self. The instrument panel presses like a steel plank against the back of my neck, pinning my right arm behind me. My head is jacked so far forward my jaw grazes my chest. I smell gasoline in my hair. I have to get out.

"What can I do?" I whimper to Jan. "My arm is stuck. I can't just lift the airplane off of me."

"Hang on. Isn't help on the way?"

"No! I have to do this myself. It's my problem to solve on my own."

"Why? What's going on?"

I don't answer.

"You insist on doing it alone?"

"I have to try." I'm sick of being dependent. I need to prove I can do it. Prove I'm worth a damn.

"But the fact is, you need some help to get out of there."

A flush of panic sweeps down my spine. It feels like I'm falling through the seat of my chair.

"Go back there," she says firmly, thumb poised to re-fire the tones. "Find some way to get help. I know you'll figure it out."

The scene is brightly lit, like a stage set or an operating theater. The cockpit I gaze into from above is scrubbed of blood and leaf debris. Rather than resting on the lawn of a suburban home, it's laid out on a concrete floor. I stand over myself lying belly up, helpless. My mind may have erased the mess, but the danger remains. I'm still trapped. I squat next to myself and grope for a handhold at the base of the broken fuselage. I grunt and heave against it. It doesn't budge. I have to get out of here. I slit my eyes for a second and see Jan on the edge of her seat, watching me. She keeps the tones playing. I take a breath and return.

"This is what we're going to do," I announce to the girl trapped in the cockpit. "I'm going to bring Jan in here to help me lift the nose of the plane. You're going to pull your arm free and get out of there."

The girl doesn't like the plan. She doesn't want to have to rely on anyone. It can make things worse.

"I know," I tell her. "I'm scared, too. But I think we can trust her." The girl blinks tears away. She nods.

One, two, and on three Jan and I lift. The girl slides out.

She stands shaking the blood back into her fingertips. Her arm is fine. Everything's fine.

"I brought you in," I tell Jan. "You helped me pick up the plane and nothing bad happened. It all turned out OK."

She laughs. "Good. Great! Thanks for letting me help."

The air around us feels swept clean and potent at the same time. Hope ripples in my chest. I feel my face crinkle into a grin.

There's just one more thing. "Let's see if accepting help in this one scenario carries over to others," she says. "Maybe now you can allow yourself to rest."

I nod. I can already sense it will work.

"Imagine you're on the couch in the living room. Find some way to relax there. Try telling yourself, 'I'm productive and need down time to stay that way.'"

I flash back to feeling hollowed out, a blank sack of nothing velcroed to the couch. I close my eyes and force myself to look around the living room again. I'm productive and need down time to stay that way. The setting sun blazes warm on my face and hands. Outside the window, a flock of starlings swarms the avocado tree. My shoulders slide away from my ears. I stretch and yawn. I pick up a book from the coffee table and settle against the cushions. I'm productive and need down time to stay that way. I check the clock. There's dinner to be made.

"How close are you to believing that you need down time?" Jan asks. "What number would you give it if ten's all the way there?"

"Maybe a seven," I tell her. "I see myself really starting to relax."

"Great. So, what's keeping it from being a ten?"

"There's this one phrase from a Bible verse Mom used to quote. 'The great cloud of witnesses.' She said that cloud was packed with all the people who set an example in their lives and went to heaven. They're looking down at us, watching what we do. They see everything."

"So you've got a celestial audience."

"Yeah, I guess so. I think for Mom it was supposed to be a positive thing, a kind of inspiration."

"But that's not what it feels like to you?"

"No. Definitely not. Ever since I was a little girl, any time I pictured that cloud I'd see my father's face. I'd see Arthur Fish. There's a big crowd behind him but he's in the front row, watching everything I do."

"Watching over you?"

"That would be nice. But no, he's not watching over me or watching out for me. He's waiting for me to do something wrong. To screw up somehow. To sin."

"He's judging you."

"He can't wait to see me fail. He wants a ringside seat. That cloud is one big panel of judges, and he's their Chief Justice."

"I notice how quick you are to pass judgment on yourself. Those witnesses must be a big part of you."

"You're right. I keep a running tally of all my fuck-ups. I hate it."

"Maybe we can use that image of the witnesses to your advantage. You could try approaching them as an adult, as your current self, and see what happens."

"Confront my inner critic?"

"Exactly. Let's try and see what comes up."

I'm sitting at my laptop, writing. The witnesses are within earshot, their cloud hovering just below the ceiling. I keep my eyes on the computer screen, trying to ignore them. But it's no use. I catch snatches of talk but can't make out full sentences. I float them a little closer and brace myself for what they're saying.

"Oh, that's good," one of them murmurs. Another agrees, "I could never do that." Their praise is so unexpected it halts my hands above the keyboard. Then my fingers begin to dip in and I'm typing again.

"Another lovely sentence!" a new voice proclaims to the group. There's a chorus of appreciative, "Ahs."

Someone shushes them. "Now she's trying to come up with a better word." They begin lobbing synonyms down to me. And just like that, they've shifted from commentators to collaborators. I go on typing and they go on feeding me suggestions, egging me on with praise. Eventually the cloud decrees I've done enough for the day. "It's time to rest so you can get more done tomorrow," they tell me.

"That's great," Jan says laughing. "You morphed them from judges into muses!"

I have my own muses. A whole crew of them. And they're not hidden in a forest glade somewhere. They're bobbing nearby, ready to help.

"How are you going to keep them accessible?" Jan wants to know.

While the tones play, my mind ties a long, long string to

the cloud. I can let my muses drift, so that when I don't need their coaching, they can be off rallying others. I watch them air-paddle away. But I don't panic. I don't need them all the time. I can trust my judgment now. About the pacing of sentences, the organization of paragraphs, the aptness of this or that metaphor. About when it's time to stop, rest and recharge. If I need their help, I can always tug on the string.

If I need Jan again, I can always pick up the phone.

•

THE FIRST ANNIVERSARY OF the airplane crash occurred on a Tuesday. After school, I walked to Dad's office and put in a couple of hours helping Mom with the filing and folding and dusting. It was already dark when we locked up and left. In the car on the way home she said, "I can't help thinking that if I hadn't miscarried before the crash, the baby would have been sitting on my lap in the plane." There would have been another child to bury. She couldn't have saved him, either.

The second and third and tenth anniversaries came and went while I was away at college, then in Paris, then grad school. I let myself forget the exact date. Mom's commemorative phone call at the end of October caught me off guard every year.

"I just wanted to let you know that Dad and I are thinking about you, today especially," she would tell me in her migraine voice, barely audible.

As the twenty-fifth anniversary approaches, I decide it's time to trade this sad ritual for something a little more celebratory. For the first time in my adult life, I am thrilled to be alive. It's been over a year since the session with Jan anchored me to my muses. I've launched my own freelance copywriting business and landed a big client for my kick-off project. Couples counseling is helping my relationship feel more viable than ever. When I catch my own reflection, more often than not I see myself as worthy, lovable. I want to welcome the next quarter century with a celebration of survival.

I rent a beach house for a weekend and invite six friends to join us. We get pulled over on the way because Matteo won't let a Mini Cooper streak past without giving chase. The state trooper tells us he clocked the Cooper doing ninety-nine miles an hour, but he lets us go because he didn't get our speed on radar. I take it as a favorable sign—bad luck turned good.

But the good luck doesn't hold. One friend arrives with a fever and makes straight for bed. Another complains he won't be able to sleep on the futon in his room. We've planned menus and hauled in enough food for an army, but disagreements flare about what to eat and when. Full-scale war breaks out on Saturday. By Sunday morning I'm down with the flu. One couple has already given up and gone home. The whole thing is a disaster. I limp home from the celebration of my new life wheezing.

A few weeks later Matteo announces that he plans to apply for a new job his company has just posted. In London. There is no return date attached. This is not another temporary gig. It's a full-fledged international move, which counts me out since he's the only one with an EU passport. Even if he asked me to go with him, I wouldn't qualify for a residency visa or a work permit. Besides, I've got my new business to run in San Francisco. I won't pick up and leave, now that I've finally got something good going. He's been talking for years about wanting to live in Europe, hankering to use all of his languages and spend more time with family there. I desperately want him beside me, especially since things are so much better between us. I want him to stay. But he wants something else. If I try to prevent him from leaving, he'll resent me.

Once the paperwork is processed, there is little time to pack and prepare. He insists this is not the end of our relationship. We are not splitting up. We meet with our couples counselor to discuss strategies for staying connected across time zones. We agree to get together every six to eight weeks. I'll take my copywriting projects to London and work on them there. And he'll be making periodic trips home for meetings at company headquarters. He fills every suitcase we own and is gone before either of us can change our minds.

After less than a week I miss him so much I wonder how I'll stand it from one month to the next. I write a long email telling him how hard it is to work and eat and sleep in our house without him there. He writes back to say that he feels the same, that on some nights he cries alone in his flat. The ache of missing him blooms into a pain I can't shake, like a rib fracture that won't knit. I count the days until I get to see him again.

•

ON THE TUBE RIDE from Heathrow, we eavesdrop on the conversations around us. Now that we're face to face again, we can't think of what to say to one another. The rest of the visit confirms how much I dislike gloomy London. But I book a flight to return two months later. On the day I arrive he is summoned to California for a meeting. I sit in his flat alone and bored, waiting for him to come back.

When he flies home to see me in San Francisco, it's for a sales kick-off at a downtown hotel. He spends most nights there with his colleagues instead of sleeping in our bed. In August, he calls from London to say he's being transferred to Munich. I fly over to help him move in the middle of a grimy heat wave. We fight from breakfast until bedtime about what to ship and what to leave, where to buy cardboard boxes and how to carry them home on the Tube.

As our one year apart stretches into two, instead of adapting to the international commute, my body clings obstinately to jet lag. During daylight hours I walk miles through German streets and parks, trying to wear myself out. But I'm still awake at dawn, the sky taut at the edges like a milk-washed tarpaulin. One insomniac morning, while he sleeps I scrounge for a blank scrap of paper to jot down the phrase I've been composing in my head over the last hour. I grab a notebook out of his briefcase and flip to the back for a clean page. I open to a list of words in a language I don't recognize. He has written the English translation next to each word. "Sweetie," "Lover," "Darling" the list begins. I don't read the rest. I'm careful to slide the notebook back where I found it, between a manila folder and a magazine. Later, in the kitchen, he pours me coffee and cream. I swallow the question in my throat. It's probably nothing.

We schedule a rendezvous in Chicago, planning a romantic

few days to ourselves before visiting family and friends. Even though our hotel bed is narrow, he manages to evade the full menu of skin I offer him. I chalk this up to jet lag and draw his smell inside me in the dark.

Before our next visit, Mom is hospitalized with a pain in her abdomen so severe she can't stand upright. Her bowel is impacted, cemented shut with colon sludge. There is little the doctors can do to offer relief. They schedule an MRI and inject dye into her arm, which swells to three times its normal size and turns black. Dad demands that she be released. I fly to Boston for Christmas and take her to see the gastroenterologist Dad selects. A needle biopsy is scheduled, the results of which are negative. The doctor explains that sometimes the needle misses the malignancy and extracts a sample of healthy tissue instead. That's what she thinks happened with Mom's biopsy. She thinks Mom has pancreatic cancer. All the signs are there. She wants to do more tests as soon as possible.

Dad rejects the lady doctor's diagnosis. He decides they'll seek a second opinion. But only after he and Mom take their annual vacation in Florida. Mom is already projectile vomiting as they pack the car for Palm Beach. She keeps it up for the full two weeks of their trip. Dad's working theory is that she contracted a parasite on a recent trip to France. He arranges an appointment with a specialist in infectious diseases, who in turn consults with his colleagues in oncology. The cancer diagnosis is confirmed.

Dad takes charge of Mom's treatment. He knows they can beat this thing. She's wracked with spasms of pain around the clock. She spends long stretches of time in the bathroom, groaning on the toilet. I hover outside the door, afraid she'll pass out from the gnashing in her gut. Dad is unsure which medications to prescribe and how much she should take. He tries opioids of different strengths, doling them out sparingly. If she's not careful, he warns, the drugs will wreck her liver.

I'm traveling constantly now, either to be with Mom on the East Coast or with Matteo in Europe. He comes to Boston a couple of times so I can see them both in the same visit. He does things that are very kind. He sits quietly beside Mom on the sofa for long stretches, despite her half-hearted attempts to shoo him away. She's embarrassed by her gas. He shrugs and tells her it's no big deal—he farts all the time himself.

I've just managed to escape to Munich for some time alone with Matteo when Sue calls with bad news. Mom's latest MRI shows lesions on all the organs of her gut. The disease is eating away her middle. He asks if I want to go to her, and I am ashamed to admit that I don't. Not at this moment. I want to breathe beside him in the dark, track the scent his head leaves on the pillow as he sweats in his sleep. But even small comforts are not to be. His cell phone rings at bed time. He doesn't pick up. When I ask why, he says it's not important. How can a ringing telephone at eleven o'clock at night be unimportant, I wonder aloud. I ask who's calling. When I press, he tells me she's a waitress in her family's restaurant. They've gone out for drinks a few times. Some nights she calls him at the end of her shift.

"It's nothing. Just drinks," he says. "I've been so lonely."

"You've been lonely? Are you serious?" I ask. "What do you

think I've been for the past two and a half years? It wasn't my idea to live this way, on separate continents!"

He doesn't answer. I picture the waitress, a dark-haired student with a hoarse laugh and no history of depression, no dying mother, no strings attached. I imagine the confident way she cocks her head when she's listening to him. How would she react to being diminished in this way, to hearing him call whatever has passed between them nothing?

"I don't know if we can make it through this," I am astonished to hear myself say.

"I don't either," he responds.

·

THREE YEARS AFTER WE packed his things for London, he moves home to San Francisco. Sue phones to tell us Mom is in the hospital. The doctors won't say how long she has left before the feasting cells finish her off. It could be hours. It could be weeks.

"Maybe she'll rally," I tell him.

"Maybe," he says. "But you should go to Boston just in case." I'm grateful he can think straight at a time when my brain has come uncabled.

Bruce's flight arrives at Logan airport an hour before mine. We meet outside baggage claim, where our niece Jacki is waiting to drive us through rush hour traffic to Emerson Hospital. I haven't been there since high school, when I was wheeled off the Children's Ward with two black eyes and no broken bones. I call Sue to update her as we inch along the gridlocked interstate. She's with Dad at Mom's bedside. A handful of family friends are there, too. Mom is unconscious, but Sue holds the phone up to her ear so I can tell her we're on our way. Bruce sings into the receiver. She's still breathing when we arrive. She lets us sit with her for a few hours before she stops.

Matteo flies in the day before her funeral. He keeps his arm tight around my shoulders throughout the long memorial service, passes me tissues, cries when I cry. That night, Mom slips into our room, draws a chair up to the bed and leans her boney weight against my shoulder. My own sobbing wakes me and I can't make it stop, can't shake the impression of her wasted frame pressed into my flesh. He spoons me tight, our heads on one pillow.

And then his sympathy dries up. It's been weeks since the funeral, he points out, but I am still sad all the time. He wants to know why I can't focus on the positive things. Mom led a comfortable life, he says, and had her family around her when she died. He can't be serious. I'm supposed to bounce back overnight? But I stop myself from snapping at him. I can't afford to lose anyone else. I ask him to be patient. I need him beside me as I stumble toward some kind of footing, some way to walk motherless in the world. He shrugs and turns away.

I fly to Boston so Sue and I can sort through Mom's things. When I get back he tells me that having the house to himself felt like being let out of prison. Like the warden skipped town.

"And look at this place," he sneers. "It's worse than a hospital."

He detests the tonics and supplements crowding the kitchen counter. It's true. I've become obsessed with my health. Mom's death was so painful she needed doses of morphine big enough to drop a linebacker. She'd only been buried a day when Dad began telling me I'd better be careful, pointing out the ways I'm at risk for a similar fate. I feel skinned alive, my nerves exposed. Stress has emptied every pocket of my body's reserves. I need all the pills and potions I can get my hands on to recuperate, to hold death at bay. Our couples therapist brokers a compromise. I keep the pill bottles but move them to a low cabinet where he doesn't have to look at them.

He starts seeing a new therapist. He wants to devote his time to individual sessions for a while. We can resume our couples work later, he says. In the meantime, he schedules an extended trip to Europe. He has a mountain of vacation time to use up. He doesn't ask me to join him. The day before his return, I'm reaching for the stapler on his desk when my eye falls on a stack of printouts. Test results. He's been taking medication for high blood pressure for more than a year, and recently met with a new doctor. Scanning the top sheet for numbers, I can't make heads or tails of it. Instead of the systolic and diastolic ratios, resting heart rate and cholesterol levels I'm expecting, I find that his HIV screen has come back non-reactive. That he tests negative for syphilis and gonorrhea.

To feel relieved and betrayed in the same moment is bizarre, like burning up and freezing at once. Since he doesn't have an STD, he probably hasn't given one to me. But why did he get tested in the first place? There's no need, unless he's having sex with someone else.

I book an emergency appointment with our couples counselor. I send a text telling him not to come home when he lands in San Francisco, but to meet me at our therapist's office. When I get there, the black smoke of his fury fills the waiting room. He can't believe I would pull a stunt like this. I tell him I won't discuss it without our therapist. In her office, I produce the test results and ask him to explain.

"Carol, what question are you asking?" our counselor wants to know.

"I'm asking why a person in a long-term monogamous relationship would need to be tested for STDs."

He growls that his doctor ordered the tests because it's standard for new patients. I turn to the therapist for confirmation that this bluff is an insult.

"That sounds reasonable," she says. "But I think the real question is, are you cheating on Carol?"

"No," he answers.

I don't believe him. But there's no way to argue. It doesn't matter that I find his explanation preposterous. He could have told his doctor not to bother with the tests. That there was no need. But he didn't. The air in the room hangs as toxic as before. Who knows what's real between us? The only thing I'm sure of is that he hates me. He can't mask it any longer. It's graffitied all over his face.

I rent a cabin in the redwoods to get away from his contempt for a week. There are books I need to sit with in solitude, books about anger and courage. I tell him it's a writing retreat. On my second day alone I notice the gunk in my lungs breaking up. By the fourth day it's as though I've escaped gravity and stepped onto a platform of air. On the sixth day I write in my journal, "Time to get out." He won't be the one to say we are finished, no matter how deeply he despises me. I have to do it.

•

THE FIRST TIME WE had sex was on Halloween. Since we never married, that became our anniversary. A few weeks shy of our twentieth Halloween together, on a Sunday morning so whited out with fog I can't see the tree outside our window, I am standing in the kitchen. One hand braced against the counter, the other struggling to grip my coffee cup. I swallow a fistful of valerian to stop hyperventilating. When I am able to speak, I tell him I can't keep doing this. Living this way. We have to separate. He guides me to the couch, sits me down, clutches my hand. We huddle together and sob for the better part of the day, tipped against one another like headstones.

Once I have declared out loud that we are finished, the rush of tenderness between us makes it hard to leave. On a yellow legal pad we list in two columns the things I'll take with me and the things he'll keep. I start sorting half-heartedly through our stuff.

This is when the evidence begins to appear. It spills out from between the spines of books on untouched shelves, from folders in ignored file drawers. He has been keeping notes for years on sheets of paper folded into sixths and eighths, every panel crammed with handwriting. I iron the creases with my palm and try to piece together a timeline from one scrap to the next. It's like a journal, each entry stashed in a separate hiding place. Some are just bullet points, scribbled on the backs of ATM receipts, dry cleaning claim checks, parking stubs. Each one reveals more about his cheating. Hook-ups with women he found online. Dates with his colleague in Silicon Valley long after he said they'd stopped meeting. His plan, during our trial separation, to fly his phone flame to San Francisco for a visit, hoping she'd agree to move in with him.

On and on it goes, confirming the suspicions I voiced during years of couples counseling. All of which he denied.

The trail goes cold right before his move overseas, but I'm convinced there is more. I go looking for it. In his briefcase I find a Hallmark card from a Dutch girl who writes how adorable he was when he picked her up on the street in Amsterdam. She loved that he bicycled around and around the Dam Square working up the nerve to talk to her. I find photographs of the two of them cuddling in a pub, and one of her beside a flowerbed in Munich's English Garden. In another card, she praises his passion as a lover and a business man.

I check his laptop. There's an ongoing email exchange with his co-worker in Italy. A guy who came to visit us in San Francisco. A guy I cooked for and laughed with and considered a friend. He's giving Matteo advice about the best places near Milan for a romantic weekend getaway with his girlfriend. They don't name names. They don't need to. Whoever she is, it's clear they've done this before. I recall the sailing trip last summer that he'd been so excited to take, the eight-course meal in Amsterdam a year ago, the weekend in Geneva. All the adventures he eagerly shared over the phone while we were living an ocean apart. All the times I only got half the story.

There is a sick that won't budge. I kneel at the toilet trying to heave it loose. But it's nailed to my gut, shuddering like the thump of an animal heart. Every solid surface I touch falls away. The tile beneath my knees, the door sill I clutch to still the spinning. Nothing about our love is true but this: I am a fucking imbecile. A puppy-eyed moron standing by her man, lapping up his lies, ravenous for any scrap faint with his scent. To hold, at last, irrefutable proof of what I've suspected and suppressed for years is not to triumph, but to writhe in shame. I have no defense. I let myself be made a gullible cunt. He watched it happening, a slow-motion swan dive into a sewer pit. He despised me for it and kept going. Now it will never be possible to imagine a single moment of our two decades together that isn't spattered in shit. I gag over the toilet again, then fall back against the sink panting.

Something digs in beside the knot of teeth and toenails and mange burrowed in my intestines. It plants a pair of steel-toed boots and slowly draws itself upright.

Rat-faced lying sack of pus! it howls.

Spineless bimbo fucker!

Miserable slithering asshole!

Anger has stomped to my rescue. It snatches me off the bathroom floor and whirls me in a funnel cloud of rending and packing. It rockets me out the door. This time for good.

IV.
RESPONSIBLE GIRL

I UNWRAP DISHES AND wine glasses, singing my head off in the kitchen, drowning out Aretha. My new loft is pristine, nothing smudged or scuffed. Now that my possessions are lighter by half, everything that's left feels essential. It all belongs. But sometimes I wake up trembling in the sulphur-orange city dark, shaking the bed. I don't know how to do this. How to be the person who lives here alone.

It's still dark when I call Dad in Boston. I climb back under the covers to break the news. My relationship is finished, I tell him. I'm on my own. There's silence on the other end of the line. Then a long exhale.

"I hear what you're saying," he says eventually. "But I can't believe it's true." He doesn't ask why I left. He doesn't ask how I'm doing. He doesn't ask if there's some way he can help.

"I just can't talk about this right now," he says. "It's too upsetting."

We hang up.

Work is a useful distraction. I do my job, keep my business running and projects coming in. But that doesn't settle me.

Some days the panic is tolerable. Most days it's not. My chief accomplishment might be downing a whole bottle of wine or binge-watching a season of "Charlie's Angels" online.

Friends drop by. They coax me out of the loft for coffee, for walks in my new neighborhood. The weeks slink past. I feel spackled to a wall of ground glass.

"I'm glad you came in," Jan says. "Sounds like things have been rough."

I'm already tearing up.

She says, "It's going to be hard for a while. But that relationship had to end before you could finish the work you started here. I know it wasn't easy to leave. I'm proud of you."

My face and hands go hot. "There's nothing to be proud of," I tell her. "He may have cheated, but it was only because I fucked things up first. I didn't make enough money. I was depressed. I got fat."

I've been spinning over and over the same ground, getting no traction. When I'm not flogging myself, I'm delivering speeches in my head, reading him the riot act. But I always come back to the same thing. It was my fault.

"Let's see if we can get to the bottom of this," Jan says.

It's been more than three years since we've done EMDR therapy together. She's got different equipment now, two vibrating touch pads, each about the size of a quarter. She has me hold them loosely in my palms, hands resting on my thighs. She adjusts the tempo. They buzz gently from one hand to the other.

"Think of a time in your relationship when you felt like a

failure. There are probably lots of examples. Just pick one." She starts the pads vibrating.

I flash to the last vacation we took together, a gorgeous, miserable week on a hilltop in Umbria, where he scrupulously avoided even the slightest touch, and where I finally slipped into an empty room in the dead of night to masturbate and cry. I shudder and flip back further, to our first Silicon Valley holiday party. His company rented the entire ground floor of a hotel. There were roulette tables in the lobby and ice sculptures on the sushi bar. The sequined sack I wore did nothing to conceal how desperately I despised my sad, matronly body. He led me to the dance floor after dinner, even though he really wanted to join one of the private parties in the suites upstairs. Halfway through the first song, he stepped away shaking his head. I couldn't get the movements right. No one had ever asked me to slow dance before.

I cast further. The scorched garlic smell of our Chicago kitchen. We're sitting around the dinner table with friends when one of them asks what made him fall in love with me. Without hesitation he answers, "She had a rockin' body." This remark comes at a point in the relationship when our nightly Haagen Dazs habit has taken its toll. It's painfully clear to everyone around the table that I no longer have a rockin' body. In the silence that follows, I light a cigarette and take a famished drag. Then I offer after-dinner drinks. The conversation lurches back to life.

"So, what's the belief?" Jan asks. "What are you telling yourself when you replay these scenes?"

"I'm disgusting," I answer. "He doesn't love me, and I have

no one to blame but myself."

"Go with that," she tells me.

What did I do wrong this time? One minute we're mopping up the last bits of a perfect meal and the next he's carving into me with a razor blade. Right there in front of our friends. I want to disappear. I want the exhalation from my cigarette to be the wisp of my body turned to vapor.

"I know I'm supposed to be angry with him," I tell Jan. "But all I can do is hate myself."

"That's OK. Stay with it."

Back at the table, the seating configuration has changed. Now I'm next to Matteo instead of across from him. When he turns to look at me, it's with a face I hardly recognize. Or two faces really, one superimposed over the other. The shadow face has reptile eyes, a flickering tongue, a flared cobra hood. There's a snake inside of him. The body coils in his belly. The blunt head stretches up through his wind pipe, poised to strike. Why haven't I seen it before? It lives there, meaty as an arm. Feeding. Molting. Warehousing venom.

"I've been trying to get him to love me," I tell Jan. "But there's a snake living inside of him. A snake with fangs."

"That sounds really dangerous."

"It is. When I wasn't who he wanted me to be, when I wasn't good enough, that snake lashed out."

"Which was a lot of the time."

"I couldn't stop him. I tried everything."

"Now that you've seen this snake and know what it's capable of, instead of trying to tame it, can you find some way to protect yourself?"

I close my eyes. We're finishing the wine. I haven't gotten up yet to clear our plates. From across the table, in her Carolina drawl, Leslie asks what made him fall in love with me. This time, when his shadow snake recoils to strike, I'm prepared. I brace my feet and buck my chair backwards, out of range. Then I swoop around the table, pulling my friends to safety. We huddle on the back porch eyeing him through the window.

Jan leaves the touch pads buzzing.

The scene shifts. I'm in an auditorium, alone among rows of empty seats. Matteo and my two fathers, Arthur Fish and Dad, stand on stage under a bank of floodlights. There's a snake inside each one of them. Three lizard faces with black beads for eyes stare out at me from behind human features.

"All right. You've got them lined up in front of you," Jan says. "What happens now?"

I keep my distance and address them one by one.

"Arthur Fish," I say. "You're sick. You trashed everyone who tried to love you." He stalks to the edge of the stage. I stand my ground. "You punished me for things I didn't do. You scared me to death. You did it on purpose. You broke my sister in two. I don't forgive you."

"Good work," Jan says. "Keep going."

"You lie. You lie!" I scream at Matteo. He looks away. "You swore you'd never hurt me. Then you clubbed my heart to a pulp. Slowly and deliberately, lie after lie. I hated myself and you just made it worse. But I finally figured it out. I'm done with you."

I turn to Dad.

"What kind of father tells his daughter he wishes she was dead?" He shrugs. "I'm sorry Nancy died. But there's no way I'm going to make up for that. You refuse to see what's good in me. Nothing I do is enough. Look at me. Look at me! I'm right here. I don't care if you want me dead. I'm alive."

I turn on my heels, march up the aisle, kick open the auditorium doors and stomp off into the night.

"They were supposed to love me," I tell Jan. "It's not my fault they couldn't, or wouldn't."

"That's right," she says. "They withheld their love all on their own. There's nothing you can do to get some people to love you. You can try, and you've definitely been trying. But in the end, it's just wasted effort."

"I feel like I've been trying my whole life. Trying and failing. And I'll never get those years back."

"True. But now you can channel that energy into being alive instead."

I cup the touch pads and pull deep drags of breath into my center. I've been wasting my time. I could never make them love me. Something migrates into my low belly. Something like grief, a blameless sadness for the girl who nearly killed herself trying.

•

I'VE STARTED WRITING ABOUT the crash again. Only now, for

the first time, I'm interested in getting beyond the family story, which is basically Dad's account of what happened. He saw streetlights below and mistook them for landing lights, in his carbon monoxide-induced stupor. When he came to, Nancy's legs were dangling lifeless beside him. He ordered Mom out. She crawled on her belly to a tree. He ordered me out, too, but my arm wouldn't budge. Then the firemen came. Police. Reporters. What did they see? There must be some kind of paper trail. Emergency response records or a police file. For the first time since the crash, I go looking.

It takes all of three mouse clicks to find the Concord Fire Department website. I type a quick email to the station chief, figuring it's a shot in the dark. He responds the same day. He tells me his department doesn't have a duty log from that time, but there may be a police report, if their files go back that far. He tells me one of his captains remembers our crash. In fact, he was one of the responders on scene that night. The chief includes an email address and phone number for this captain, along with his shift schedule and permission to call him at work.

It's all too much to process sitting down. I pace the eleven steps it takes to cross my kitchen and the eleven to return until my ears finally quit clanging. I freeze mid-stride, seized by the idea that I've been thrown a rope. Looking down, I see my hands gripping so frantically the knuckles pop through skin. I dial Concord.

Captain Prentiss is a no-nonsense guy. He launches right in with what he remembers. He and a partner were assigned to an ambulance that night. They had just dropped off a patient at Emerson Hospital when the first transmission came over the radio. All personnel were to stand by for a possible downed plane. He and his partner left the hospital and drove in the direction of Hanscom Field. They were already in the neighborhood when the location of the crash was broadcast. Theirs was the first ambulance to arrive at the Monsen Road address. They set up triage and began pulling people out. First was the young girl strapped into her seat, he tells me. They cut her loose, stabilized her spine and loaded her into one of the waiting ambulances. The second person, an adult, was outside the plane and had lost a lot of blood. Male or female, he can't remember. Just that they had deep wounds to the face and legs.

"You stabilized the girl's spine?" I have to ask. "Was she—?" I can't say it. Was she still alive?

He doesn't answer directly. I can't tell if this is due to gaps in his memory or out of simple compassion. He informs me that all of the passengers would have been whipped forward on impact, flung back, then thrown forward again when the fuselage flipped upside-down. In that circumstance, with the head snapping back and forth, a spine board is standard procedure.

"After that, it's pretty murky," he says. He recalls just scattered details. They had to post an all-night fire watch on the crash site until the FAA could haul the wreckage away. He tells me he checked the police department for a record of Nancy's death but didn't find anything. He assumes the FAA took that, too, for their investigation.

"Investigation?" I ask.

"It's routine in aviation," he says. "Light aircraft get the same treatment as commercial airliners. They investigate every case."

I flash to Dad sitting up in bed, propped against a tower of pillows, one arm in a sling. There are files lying open on the bedspread. He balances a clipboard on his lap, one of his fussy fountain pens poised over a sheet of paper. He's writing a letter to the FAA. "They want to ruin me," he mutters more than once before the letter gets sent.

"Matter of fact, I remember the investigator," Captain Prentiss is saying. "He told us how tough that aircraft was. If he'd had to crash a light plane, the Navion was the one he'd have chosen. Nothing else could've taken that kind of beating."

My lips move, but I can't make words.

"The investigation files are public," he continues. "I think you can even look them up online. The NTSB keeps all those records."

It's impossible to convey to him how grateful I am. For what he remembers. For holding Nancy's head so carefully while they freed her from the wreck. He bats away my thanks and asks me to call again if he can help in any other way. We hang up. I stare at the receiver in my palm.

It takes a bit of digging on the National Transportation Safety Board website, but eventually I find what I'm looking for: a searchable database of accident investigations, catalogued by year and month. I scroll to 1979 and click on October. Ours is last in the list of twelve planes that crashed on Sunday, October 28th. Eleven of the twelve crashes that day were nonfatal.

I click a button marked Probable Cause and a one-page

synopsis of the investigation results pops up on screen. My eye skims over the location and date of the crash, aircraft data, purpose of the flight, pilot data, type of accident. Halfway down the page, in the field designating probable cause, I read "pilot in command" and "improper IFR operation." I blink and read the line again. Pilot in command. That means Dad. And IFR operation has something to do with the plane's instruments. What the hell? I race through the list of contributing factors, forgetting to breathe. The first reads, "Attempted operation with known deficiencies in equipment." The second points to a problem with something called the directional gyroscope. The remaining factors all pertain to weather. Low ceiling, fog, icing conditions. That's it. No mention of carbon monoxide.

I don't understand. The official record omits the most important factor, the central tenet of the story. We were slowly knocked unconscious by the gas. Dad resisted as long as he could. He got us within minutes of the runway. We almost made it. But the screen in front of me doesn't mention any of this.

I clap my hand over my mouth. They think Dad was at fault. They're saying he didn't follow procedure. Something was wrong with the plane, but he flew anyway.

The full report is eighty-six pages long. The woman on the phone in Washington, D.C. asks if I'd like copies of the photographs as well, for an additional fee. I read her my credit card number. She tells me the file will arrive in three weeks. I don't know how I'll be able to wait that long. I need to get to the bottom of this. So I go on digging.

A reference librarian at the Concord Public Library assures me they have issues of the local newspapers from 1979 on microfilm. Since I can't do it myself, I ask Sue to help me find clippings about the crash. She pores over reel after reel, feeding quarters into the machine to make photocopies. It's the pictures accompanying these articles that are especially hard to take. Even fuzzed out by the library's copy machine, they're still astonishing. My brain can't piece together an airplane from the tableau of fragments. There's a wheel, a partial tail number. There's the tree Mom must have dragged herself to. There's a fireman pointing a hose at the pulped snout of the fuselage. Somewhere behind that they found me. Then they found my arm. I look and look, but I don't see how a whole person could have emerged from such bedlam.

The last item in the stack of copies is the weekly Police Blotter printed in the *Concord Journal* four days after the accident:

> The fatal crash of a light aircraft on Monsen Road at 6 p.m. Sunday evening, in which a 12-year-old Carlisle girl died, brought forth all elements of the local Police and Fire Departments.
>
> The Concord Fire Department, directed by Chief Richard Ryan and Captain Stanley Orpik, coordinated the rescue efforts while Firefighter Bill Robinson operated the "Jaws of Life" with such expertise that he was able to do in a matter of minutes what Police and Firefighters were unable to do physically for nearly one half hour. We are referring to the freeing of one of the victims, Carol Miller, 16, who was trapped under the

dashboard of the aircraft.

The police, directed by Sgt. John T. Foster, assisted in the removal of all four victims, while Officers Scott Comeau and Kevin Walsh stayed in or near the plane constantly, encouraging the trapped young girl while gasoline dripped over and around them.

All three officers received commendations for their efforts.

If I close my eyes I can smell raw fuel, hear Dad hollering at me to get out, as if I'd done something wrong. "Daddy," I called. He didn't respond. Then the bright-haired man was asking questions. His voice quavered. He was scared, too. The gasoline was everywhere. But he stayed with me in the dark until my arm slipped free.

•

THE UPS DRIVER DELIVERS a heavy envelope from D.C. I cradle it in my left arm to sign and almost drop it on my foot. Before the door swings shut I'm already ripping into it. I shake a fat sheaf of pages onto the kitchen table and flip first to the pictures. They're indecipherable, reduced by a government Xerox machine to abstract patches of black and white. I pace a few fast laps from table to sink and back, flicking nerves off my fingertips. I chug two glasses of water, wipe the rim and set the glass in the dish drainer. Then there's nothing to do but start reading.

A quarter of the report is dedicated to hieroglyphic strings of weather data. I wade through statements signed by air traffic control personnel. There is an audit of the landing system, a graph of the sixty-foot debris field, an inventory of the damages. Left wing, demolished. Left flap, demolished. Right wing, right flap, demolished. Fuel system, oil system, electrical system, hydraulic system, all demolished. I turn to the two narrative accounts of the crash. The one submitted by Dad is called a Pilot Aircraft Accident Report. The one written by the FAA investigator is called a Factual Aircraft Accident Report. That only one of these is labeled factual makes the hair on the back of my neck stand up.

The factual report concludes that there were no equipment failures during the flight except for the directional gyroscope, one of the instruments essential for navigation. The inspector notes that the gyroscope was known to be malfunctioning prior to our flight. In Dad's report, he acknowledges that the gyroscope was faulty. It required frequent corrections—sometimes by as much as thirty degrees—during the return trip. But he dismisses this as a minor concern, insisting he's too experienced a pilot for that kind of hiccup to have caused the crash. "No accident would have occurred," he writes, "if there had not been exhaust leakage to the cabin." Under the circumstances, he did everything right. He was breathing poison gas. Carbon monoxide exposure should be considered the sole cause of the crash.

I toss my glasses onto the fan of pages and press my face into my palms. Dad never makes mistakes. Of course. Other people do. The surgeons who stitched him back together so carelessly. The paramedics who assumed Mom was thrown from the plane. The FAA investigator who took him for some kind of rookie. In the pilot's report, Dad sets the record straight. He could've landed that plane with his eyes closed. He didn't screw up. The crash wasn't his fault.

Maybe that's why I thought it was mine. Somebody had to take responsibility. He wasn't offering, so I volunteered. I lined up the facts I needed to make my case. Fact one: I convinced Dad to fly that day. Fact two: I asked for the heat, which unleashed the lethal gas and led to fact three: I killed my sister. I've been tying myself in knots for three decades, frantic to implicate myself. Letting Dad off the hook. Why? He hasn't done the same for me. He would never admit that he took a risk flying with faulty equipment, never entertain the possibility that he made a fatal error. Not even to help his surviving daughter feel less wretched.

I push away from the table to stand at the sliding glass door. The patio is covered in thick drifts of bamboo leaves. Their tannins have leached into the concrete, leaving tea-colored stains shaped like knives.

I stay on my feet to scan what's left. The transcript of final radio communications between Dad and the control towers at Logan Airport and Hanscom Field, where we were supposed to land, gives a minute-by-minute countdown to the crash. We're there one minute and gone the next.

(5:28pm)

Dad: "Hanscom Tower, this is Navion Two-Four-One-Two-Tango inbound."

Hanscom Tower, Bedford: "Navion One-Two-Tango, this is Hanscom Tower. Report the marker inbound."

Dad: "Will do."

(5:29pm)

(5:30pm)

Dad: "One-Two-Tango reporting outer marker inbound."

Hanscom: "One-Two-Tango cleared to land runway One-One. Report the field in sight."

Dad: "One-Two-Tango."

(5:31pm)

(5:32pm)

(5:33pm)

(5:34pm)

(5:35pm)

Logan Tower, Boston: "Hanscom, you got landing assured on One-Two-Tango?"

Hanscom: "Negative, don't see him. We're not talking to him either."

Logan: "You're—you haven't talked to him?"

Hanscom: "We have. We're not talking to him now."

Logan: "Hmm. We don't have him."

Hanscom: "Uh, let's try him again. Hang on. . . . Why don't you try him. We're not, uh, we're not talking to him."

Logan: "We'll give him another shot. . . ."

(5:36pm)

Logan: "And we—we tried him. He's not on the frequency. Any chance he's on the field and you haven't spotted him yet?"

Hanscom: "No, we don't see him at all. . . . And we're not talking to that One-Two-Tango at all. We don't see him on the airport and he's not on ground frequency at all."

(5:37pm)

Logan: "Okay. We don't have a target around the airport and we're not talking to him."

Hanscom: "Roger."

Those five minutes of dead air on the page terrify me. I've tried, but I can't remember diving through the trees, hitting the ground, flipping over. It's like I didn't exist for that slice of time. Whenever I've pictured it, Dad is passed out, slumped over the controls. Now I imagine him awake in the moments before we hit. Messing with the gyroscope, maybe making one last correction. Anything could have happened.

•

I DON'T KNOW WHICH story to believe. In the official version, Dad is reckless. In mine, he's a victim of my selfishness. In Dad's, the responsibility never lands on him. He has assembled a list of scapegoats over the years, but lately he's taken to blaming demons. The way he tells it these days, there were evil forces at work in the cockpit during our fatal flight. Demonic forces summoned by Arthur Fish. My dead father supposedly reached back from beyond the grave intent on destroying Dad's life. In fact, ever since Dad married Mom, Arthur Fish has been plotting against him. Even in the afterlife he's insane with jealousy. Dad snagged his young widow, so he's bent on revenge.

I first heard about these maleficent powers a few years ago, when Mom and Dad were moving into a new house. Dad was unpacking boxes. He turned abruptly and tripped over the open drawer of a filing cabinet. Arthur Fish opened that file drawer, Dad said. It had been closed a moment before. He did it to hurt Dad. Just like the day of the plane crash. Arthur Fish jammed the airplane's heater switch so it couldn't be turned off. He's the one who released poisoned gas into the cabin. His wickedness will stop at nothing. Since he failed to kill Dad in the plane, demonic Arthur Fish gave Mom cancer to steal her away.

I'm on the move again, clocking fast laps between the table and the sink.

Holy shit! This is the man we put in charge of our lives. Our pilot in command. He spews this craziness, spins this outrageous web of denial. He tells me I should have died in the crash. And still I try to get him to act like a father, to protect me and make me safe. What was I thinking? I can hear Mom's repeated assurances. "He knows what he's doing," she promised. "He would never let anything happen to us." But something did happen. He almost killed us all. Instead of owning up to it, he pins it on a ghost.

I understand that remorse can take a terrible toll on the mind. That a certain kind of madness gets wrung from grief. But if it were remorse Dad felt for flying on faulty instruments, surely he would have apologized by now. Even once.

I stop pacing. Dad's not the only one who skips the "I'm sorrys." No wonder I chose the partner I did. Matteo has no appetite for accountability either. They both push their plates away. They sit back and watch while I castigate myself for their mistakes. It seems so obvious, but I never noticed the pattern before. It just felt like home, cozying up to someone who couldn't cop to his own bad behavior. Someone who'd rather sit through years of couples therapy than come clean. Someone who accuses me of imprisoning him, then refuses to say we're done. Admitting our relationship was dead would have meant facing the part he played in killing it.

A few months ago, a friend ran into Matteo in an airport. She asked him why we'd split up. She wanted to hear what he had to say. He shrugged. "Carol had a bad year," he told her. End of story. His double life, his massive cache of lies played no part. The breakup was all my doing.

I chose him because he was deeply familiar. I clung to him until the bitter end because he confirmed the essential things I'd been raised to know about myself: I was less than. And I was to blame. With someone like that, I didn't stand a chance.

But that's OK. I'm OK, I tell myself, sinking into a chair. I made it through. I'm starting to see my patterns. I'm learning to pull myself out of harm's way, to spot the difference between contempt and love. I'm no longer the girl who lives in their houses, who sees herself diminished to a scribble. I'm no longer the girl who stays.

My gaze travels around the loft. Everything here is me. The thirty-one cartons of books on their shelves. The desk attended by a cloud of muses. The watermelon-red table with its collection of mismatched chairs. This is my place. I'm the one who'll decide where the story goes from here. The one responsible for my next breath, and the next.

EPILOGUE: LIFT

AN ALARM CLOCK BLEATS in the five a.m. dark, rolling me onto my back. The headlights of a solitary car sweep the ceiling, casting silhouettes of trees that my sleeping brain can somehow still name. Sequoia. Washingtonia palm. Live oak. Country trees, not urban ones. Where am I? I turn to the middle of the bed, the pillowcase cold against my cheek. Our noses almost touch. Even in the dark I can tell how broadly he's smiling, with every muscle in his face.

"Congratulations," he whispers, and my mind stirs to a gallop.

This is it. Today!

"Thank you for being alive," he says. He kisses me slowly, like we've got all day. Then he whips off the covers.

"Time to get up!" he laughs. "Can't be late."

•

I FOUND HIM ONLINE. I didn't believe it could happen on some cheesy website, but friends kept nudging me in that direction. "When you're ready," they'd say during one of our walks in the Presidio or Golden Gate Park. To play along, I'd pull up the most popular dating site and page through faces. I called this "looking at the dudes" and went on looking for a year. I needed time to do my research. I studied blog posts on how to gin up an irresistible dating profile and exploit the site's arsenal of winks, blinks, whistles, clicks and slaps. I compared wish-list strategies and read cautionary tales about in-person dates. When I felt close to ready, I drafted a bio and revised it seven times. I agonized over every descriptor. Was I curvy, or was that a euphemism for fat? Should I call myself a social drinker or an occasional one? It took a month to curate a collection of stamp-sized photographs. If I only posted head shots, would the dudes automatically assume I was grotesque from the neck down?

When my profile finally went live, the magic of the site algorithm kicked in. I started receiving daily emails with lists of potential dates. "Carol! You like dogs but don't own one," a message began. "Bill is a dog owner and he's looking for you!" It didn't take long to catch on. I'd been sweating over the selection criteria for nothing. "You like good food and so does Tom!" "You and James both listen to music!"

Women on the site were expected to stick to the sidelines, post cute photos of ourselves and wait for the men to come to us. Because I couldn't stomach sitting around hoping that a dude would make a move, I sent messages to guys whose profiles struck a chord. By the end of week two, I'd traded emails with half a dozen and booked a live coffee date. I wanted very much to like him in person. I felt no zap of attraction when we shook hands, but he was interesting and genuine and easy to talk to. We chatted for more than an hour. I kept willing the needle on my excitement meter to budge. It just sat there. He wanted to see me again, and pressed for a real date. I demurred. He moved in to kiss me goodbye and, on reflex, I offered my cheek. Back home, I kicked off my shoes and pulled the comforter over my head. This was going to take a very long time. Maybe forever. The odds of a straight woman over forty finding her mate in San Francisco were ridiculously grim.

I spent the afternoon brooding. Eventually I shoveled myself out from beneath the covers and went to meet friends for dinner. They expected a full report. When I didn't conceal my discouragement, they gave me the climb-back-on-the-bicycle talk. I couldn't abandon all hope on the basis of a single lukewarm coffee date, they argued. The hardest part was behind me, now that I'd jumped into the fray. I promised that I'd log in when I got home and contact at least one new dude before heading to bed.

That took some doing. The same faces kept cropping up, no matter how often I refreshed the browser. I had already run through the roster multiple times, agonizing over whether I was giving each tiny head shot a fair shake. I decided to extend my search parameters. Instead of dudes living within fifty miles of San Francisco, I increased it to seventy-five. It worked. Those twenty-five extra miles pulled in a whole slew of new faces. I wrote a quick note to a divorced high school English teacher and gave myself permission to log off. Then I poured myself some wine and decided I might as well scan the rest of the search results.

It was his mouth that brought my scrolling finger to a screeching halt. Full lips framed by perfect parentheses. I studied that mouth hungrily, cackling into my wine glass. I scanned his vitals. Two years younger and two inches taller than me. Divorced with two kids. Living alone in a cute town in wine country. His description of himself began, "I am a therapist and a writer." That's when I stopped breathing.

His turned out to be the best piece of writing I'd seen in twelve months of dude looking. It outshone the others' efforts so brilliantly I winced for them. I had to contact him, if for no other reason than to congratulate him on crafting the profile to end all profiles. Besides, he was actively seeking email. "Be bold," his bio pleaded. "Write first. It drives me crazy to think I might miss you." So I wrote, warning myself not to expect a reply even as I slipped in what I hoped would be a few tantalizing facts about myself. I mentioned that I was writing about EMDR. It seemed like a therapist would take that bait.

I woke late the next morning, Labor Day. No plans or projects beckoned. When I got around to checking email, his reply had been sitting in my inbox for almost twelve hours. He'd sent it at one o'clock in the morning, to let me know that he was free all day. He offered to drive into San Francisco so we could meet.

My nonchalant reply took an hour to craft. Sure, I'd be up for grabbing coffee that afternoon, if he was coming into town. I also let him know I had a meeting scheduled with a client in wine country the next day. If not today, I suggested, maybe we could get together tomorrow. I included my phone number in case he felt like talking instead of emailing. The phone rang a few minutes later.

"Wow! You have a great voice," he said, after we'd traded hellos.

"You're kidding," I laughed. Was he putting me on? I'd always thought my speaking voice was nasal and adolescent sounding. Whenever I'd sung along with the radio in the car, Matteo had bayed like a hound to shut me up. But this man liked the way I sounded. He wanted to hear everything. Where did I grow up? How had I become a writer? Why was I writing about EMDR therapy? I was usually the one firing a barrage of questions, but his curiosity easily kept pace with mine. Ten minutes into our conversation, I was hip deep in the story of the plane crash. I stopped mid-sentence, suddenly self-conscious. If I spilled my guts too fast, I'd come off sounding like just another head case, not date material.

"It's OK," he joked, reading my hesitation. "Today's a holiday. I'm not on duty."

He wanted to listen to as much of my story as I wanted to tell. Not to analyze it, but to begin to know me, to catch glimpses of what I'd come through. When he told me that he used EMDR almost daily in his psychotherapy practice, my hand actually jumped out of my lap and slapped my forehead, just like in cartoons. Nobody's going to believe this, a voice squeaked, pogoing up and down at the back of my brain.

We pried ourselves off the phone after three giddy hours of conversation. We'd agreed to meet at his loft the following evening. I emailed the address to my friend Brooke, who worried I was being reckless. I told her I didn't think he was dangerous. I was more concerned about what I might do to him. No one had touched me in years. I couldn't remember the last time desire had driven a man to reach for me. I was so overdue for some contact my skin crisped with longing. I pictured the sexy mouth of the dude who had just swooned over my voice on the phone. I'd have to find some way to keep my wits about me.

I pawed to the bottom of a dresser drawer and dug out the most embarrassing underwear I could find. The tummy-control granny panties that, out of irrational thrift, I couldn't bring myself to throw away. That's what I would wear to our first meeting, underneath my carefully chosen outfit. I could never strip down to anything so hideous in front of a potential lover. The underwear would buy me time to consult my timorous heart.

I grazed his doorbell, heard feet on the stairs and dropped my gaze to the ground, afraid to look. He opened the door and drew me into a hug.

"Can you feel how hard my heart is pounding?" he asked.

Mine tom-tommed in response. We stepped apart and looked each other fleetingly in the face. My cheeks blazed.

"Come in, Carol Fish Miller," he smiled.

I did a quick check for raised hackles before following him up a flight of stairs. He was, indeed, as tall as his profile claimed. He was leaner than I'd imagined, but his hug felt solid, substantial. The clothes he was wearing, the furniture in the rented loft, the art on the walls all suggested a compatible aesthetic. I grimaced at how superficial these things seemed, but went on with the appraisal anyway. I needed someone whose tastes hovered in the same zip code as mine.

There was a sofa and chair, but he didn't ask me to sit down. Instead, he paced. I let my shoulder bag slide to the floor and stood looking, blatantly this time, at the space. He didn't seem to notice that I was still standing at the top of the stairs. I moved three steps into the room, pulled a stool out from the breakfast bar and perched on it. Would I like some wine, he thought to ask. Ducking into the pantry to retrieve a bottle, rummaging in a drawer for the corkscrew, reaching for wine goblets on a high shelf all helped to calm him. He poured two very full glasses, carried them back around the counter and took the other stool.

We sat facing one another, flushed and grinning, slugging back Pinot. One of us would fumble the thread of conversation and we'd both reach to retrieve it, talking at the same time. He was in the middle of saying something. I was trying hard to follow. He dropped from his bar stool, closed the space between us and leaned in for a massive smooch. Then he hopped back onto his seat and declared, "You're a babe!" After that, it was impossible not to stare at his mouth. We tittered and blushed and tripped through more talk, then rose and pulled one another into a steamy clinch. He laced his fingers into mine and tugged me gently toward a second flight of stairs leading up to the bedroom.

"Come on," he said.

I froze. My hideous underwear blazed to life and can-canned before my eyes.

"I can't, even though I want to," I said, covering his hand with both of mine and backing him away from the stairs. "It's too soon."

He didn't try to topple my flimsy resolve. Instead, he asked if I liked Thai food. We kissed more, giggled more, talked more, ate noodles and satay. I drove back into the city very late, crossing the Golden Gate Bridge after midnight through dripping garlands of fog.

We had four days together before I flew to Maine for vacation. I'd been looking forward to the trip for months, but suddenly two weeks seemed far too long to be away. My flight left on Monday morning. Sunday evening I drove the sixty miles one way to steal a few hours with him. His kids had been at his loft all weekend. As soon as he dropped them off at their mother's house, he called me.

"Where are you?" he asked. "I can't wait another second!"

We took the stairs two at a time, laughing and breathless at the top, unbuttoning one another out of clothes, travelling each new stretch of skin with famished eyes and fingers. I was on intimate terms with my body's flaws, but it was impossible to misread the rapture in this man's face.

"You're a goddess," he breathed.

He emailed me every day of my vacation, several times a day. I'd wake at first light, too excited to sleep, and drive to the library parking lot to pick up a wifi signal. He wrote about what he'd seen on his morning run. He wrote comments on manuscript pages I'd drafted and sent him the day before. He wrote late-night postscripts to our evening phone calls.

I'd been wracking my brain all summer trying to come up with the best way to celebrate the thirtieth anniversary of the plane crash. It had to be jubilant, something primal and intensely pleasurable. Something that captured the euphoria of being exuberantly alive. The date was less than six weeks away and I still hadn't made plans. One night, on the phone from Maine, I asked him to join me in whatever I finally decided to do. He responded exactly as I'd hoped he would, saying he'd love to, saying he was flattered to be asked.

The next day he emailed to say he'd woken up with the perfect idea for the celebration. He'd considered just surprising me, but because there was a chance I might find it scary instead of fun, he figured he should ask first. He teased me, drawing it out, building suspense, promising to reveal all once I got back to San Francisco. When my flight arrived, he was standing as close to the gate as he could get without risking arrest.

•

WE DRESS QUICKLY IN the cold, piling on layers of wool and fleece. Then we huddle in his kitchen, blowing into hot mugs of unnecessary coffee. We're both already so awake we're trembling. We brush our teeth, pull on hats and jackets and spill out into the morning dark, our breath condensing ahead of us. He uses a kitchen spatula to scrape frost off the windshield.

Our instructions are to rendezvous with the pilot at seven o'clock. We arrive ahead of schedule and sit in the car with the heater running. At 7:01 we join the small group gathered in a corner of the parking lot. A utility van pulls up and our crew jumps out. The van is towing a trailer, onto which is lashed what looks like a Godzilla-sized Easter basket. At the sight of it, the reality of what we are about to do clips me in the wind-pipe. I lean over to steady my breathing and he's beside me instantly, one reassuring hand on my back.

"We don't have to do this," he reminds me. "Just say the word."

I shake my head. No way am I chickening out. Not today of all days.

A second van pulls alongside the first. Eight passengers pile in. We ride to a remote corner of the airfield where there is room to unfurl a massive plastic tarp and, on top of that, a building-sized swath of blinding colors. The envelope, it's called. An enormous silk windsock stitched from six-foot rect-angles of fuchsia and blue and canary yellow. The pilot stations two volunteers on either side of the opening at its base. They grip the guy wires that attach the fabric to the basket, holding the lines taut to keep the mouth from collapsing while five-foot fan blades drive a tornado of air into the envelope.

As I watch, jumping in place to stay warm, the blue time before sunrise turns salmon at the edges. The sun lifts from behind Hood Mountain just as the balloon begins to billow like a spinnaker.

The basket is partitioned into five sections: the pilot's compart-ment in the center surrounded by four two-person stalls in each of the corners. We use footholds woven into the side to climb in while the pilot fires a massive blow torch into the envelope in deafening bursts. The ground crew drops the mooring lines. A shiver shoots through the wicker and steals my breath. There's a second tremor, like the stomp of an impatient foot, followed by the brusque tug of leaving. We jostle like subway riders and bob five feet off the tarmac, unlatching gravity's grip. Then we rise. Over the white vans, the trailer, the waving crew. Over hangars and private planes, six-seaters chocked and angled in rows.

We clear the control tower on a billow of October air sharp as the bark of a fox. Each blast of the burner wafts us higher. We drift transfixed, ruddering a creaking raft above roads and houses, over a flock of goats behind a shopping mall and a yellow fleet of school buses. Nosing south and west, we slowly trade the cul-de-sacs and gated subdivisions for a patchwork of farmland and vineyards. The pilot lets hot air escape through a valve at the top of the balloon. The sound spooks a group of horses hundreds of feet beneath us. A man runs out of a barn to wave us off angrily. "Fuckers!" he shouts, and gives us the finger with both hands. We ascend again and hop a new current. I grapple for a word or a way to describe how improbable it feels to stand on the air like this, moving in complete stillness like an untethered elevator. Rising weightless, falling frictionless. Hanging brightly above what looks insurmountable from the ground.

When there is nothing below us but a sea of vermilion grapevines we descend again, skating down livid vineyard rows, flushing jackrabbits from the canopy. Later, we'll land in a fallow field. Two shy ponies and a mule will edge toward our colorful party. We'll deflate the envelope on the grass, patting out air pockets on our hands and knees. But for now, we remain impossibly aloft, a dumbfounded litter of kittens peering from a basket, the world brimming in our eyes. Beyond one final violet spine of hills the Pacific appears, a white smudge of surf slowly erasing the coast. I soar in autumn sunshine and am alive.

ACKNOWLEDGMENTS

THIS BOOK HAS BEEN so many years in the making I can only name some of those who cheered me along and kept it moving toward completion.

I am grateful to my siblings, especially Bruce and Sue, for bravery and unfailing love. You recognize me, restore me, enfold me.

Thanks to Connie Rubiano, LCSW and Jan Cehn, LCSW for healing steeped in humor and huge affection.

Thanks to Tim Schaffner for prizing serendipity and focusing this story's power, and to Brooke Johnson for your friendship and exquisite hand.

I am indebted to the early readers who answered my questions, including Lisa Awrey, Andy Church, Stacy Freed Low, JoAnne Klein, Kristyn Komarnicki Blançon, Gail Sansbury, Jacqi Tully, Rita Weisskoff, Steve Weisskoff and the astonishing Sophie Weisskoff, among others.

Thanks to the Core of Four for never losing interest, and to the Savory Tarts for relentless enthusiasm.

Praise be to Leslie Williams for showing me how to begin the telling, for accompanying me through each incarnation, for a honed eye and giving heart that let me flourish.

Thanks to Elsie and Nicco for being family. And awesome.

Without Andrew Lewis Weisskoff, my champion and collaborator, my dork at the end of the dark, this book would not be. For comfort when I was writing and crying, for deep insight into EMDR and all the rest of it, for polishing each sentence, for a hundred manifestations of love, thank you.

Further Reading on EMDR Therapy

The Body Keeps the Score: Brain, Mind, and Body in the Healing of Trauma, Bessel van der Kolk, MD, 2014, Viking Penguin.

Getting Past Your Past: Take Control of Your Life with Self-Help Techniques from EMDR Therapy, Francine Shapiro, Ph.D., 2013, Rodale Books.

The Instinct to Heal: Curing Depression, Anxiety, and Stress Without Drugs and Without Talk Therapy, David Servan-Schreiber, MD, Ph.D., 2003, Rodale Books.

Secrets, Lies, Betrayals: How the Body Holds the Secrets of a Life, and How to Unlock Them, Maggie Scarf, 2005, Ballantine Books.

Tapping In: A Step-by-Step Guide to Activating Your Healing Resources Through Bilateral Stimulation, Laurel Parnell, Ph.D., 2008, Sounds True.

Finding and evaluating an EMDR therapist:

EMDR Institute, www.EMDR.com Dual overviews of EMDR therapy for clinicians and lay readers. Guidelines for choosing a therapist trained to use the protocol and a directory of certified EMDR therapists around the world.

EMDR International Association, www.EMDRIA.org
Online home of the professional organization for EMDR practitioners includes a resources section and "Find a Therapist" tool.